Railroad Vision

Railroad Vision

Steam Era Images from the *Trains* Magazine Archive

With an Introduction by Kevin P. Keefe
Edited by Wendy Burton and Jeff Brouws

The Quantuck Lane Press / New York

For two visionary editors: Jim Mairs and David P. Morgan

Railroad Vision
Steam Era Images from the
Trains Magazine Archive

Copyright © 2015 by Jeff Brouws & Wendy Burton
Introduction © 2015 by Kevin P. Keefe
All rights reserved
Printed in China
First Edition

Book design and composition by Jeff Brouws
Editing and sequencing by Wendy Burton
Manufacturing by Asia-Pacific

Library of Congress Cataloging-in-Publication Data
Railroad vision : steam era images from the Trains magazine archive / with an introduction
by Kevin P. Keefe ; edited by Wendy Burton & Jeff Brouws. -- First edition.
     pages cm
ISBN 978-1-59372-060-5
1. Railroads--United States--History--Pictorial works. 2. Steam locomotives--United
States--Pictorial works. 3. Photography of railroads. I. Burton, Wendy, 1951- II. Brouws,
Jeffrey T. III. Trains (Milwaukee, Wis. : 1954). Selections.
TJ603.2.R335 2015
625.100973--dc23
                              2015002969

The Quantuck Lane Press | New York
www.quantucklanepress.com

Distributed by W. W. Norton & Company
500 Fifth Avenue, New York, NY 10110
www.wwnorton.com

W. W. Norton & Company Ltd., Castle House,
75/76 Wells Street, London, WIT 3QT

TITLE PAGE Canadian Pacific mixed train #659,
near Port Burwell, Ontario, September 1957.
John A. Rehor

DEDICATION PAGE Lehigh Valley 4-6-2 #2097,
Ithaca, New York, February 1941.
David R. Connors

OPPOSITE Eastbound Nickel Plate freight on
high bridge, Conneaut, Ohio, March 1957.
Jim Shaughnessy

PAGE 23 Union Pacific freight train,
Snake River Valley, Idaho, October 17, 1953.
David W. Salter

PAGE 181 Southern Pacific narrow gauge
4-6-0 #18, Laws, California, April 1956.
Wendell Mortimer

PAGE 195 Erie 2-8-2 with drag freight,
North Judson, Indiana, January 1941
C. G. Gibb

Introduction

Railroad Vision

Trains Magazine and the Evolution
of American Railroad Photography

Kevin P. Keefe

ONE OF THE MOST IMPORTANT COLLECTIONS of railroad photographs in America resides unceremoniously behind two pairs of unmarked blue doors in the middle of an office building in a western suburb of Milwaukee. You might go right past it as you walk down the muffled second-floor corridor. The only clue to what's inside is a small, framed, black-and-white portrait of a ruddy-faced, white-haired, late-middle-aged man in a characteristic dress shirt and tie, his face betraying the merest suggestion of a wry smile. Beside the portrait is a small sign: DAVID P. MORGAN MEMORIAL LIBRARY.

Modest as the doorway is, it promises wonders. Inside the 76 x 30–foot room, a skein of steel file cabinets lines the north wall, containing tens of thousands of black-and-white prints that represent a historical survey of American railroad photography. The official estimate of the number of prints for insurance purposes is 120,000. You could say the contents of those cabinets are the tangible expression of a seventy-five-year tradition of photojournalism and art. They represent the first five decades of pictures either published by or submitted to *Trains* magazine, launched by Kalmbach Publishing Co. in 1940. As such, this archive is unique and indispensable in breadth and scope.

As a physical entity, the collection won't win any awards from the Society of American Archivists. Intended as a tool to serve the needs of magazine editors and designers, it's more like an old-fashioned newspaper morgue: the prints are worked over, picked apart, thumbed and bent, sometimes even cracked. No one who works in the library has any archive training or accreditation. Editors never wear gloves. Few if any of the prints are stored in glassine envelopes. There isn't even a database to keep track of everything. The entire collection is self-catalogued; for more than a half century,

prints arrived on editors' desks, those editors and librarians eventually decided on the correct files for them, and that was that. To locate anything, a visitor has to know what to look for, and where.

So a professional archivist might be shocked. No matter. After seventy-five years, the *Trains* collection continues to serve its purpose, supplying the editors of Kalmbach publications with an unmatched variety of railroad imagery spread across more than 150 years of railroad history. It represents the collective vision of three generations of the magazine's editors and contributing photographers.

THE ARCHIVES' ORIGINAL VISIONARY was the company's founder himself, Albert C. "Al" Kalmbach. He earned an electrical engineering degree from Milwaukee's Marquette University in 1932 but also had a keen sense for publishing, having honed his skills editing and printing a quite clever neighborhood newspaper during his adolescent years on Milwaukee's west side. He was a very good writer, with a penchant for simple, pithy prose that persistently conveyed optimism. When, it is said, an engineering job with the Pennsylvania Railroad didn't pan out after graduation, the self-reliant Kalmbach instead turned to something he knew, creating

Model Railroader magazine in January 1934. Whether he started the magazine out of a love for model railroading or for publishing is anyone's guess. Whatever his motivation, a good model railroad magazine would require good prototype photography, and so it was that a modest collection of black-and-white pictures began to take shape.

Kalmbach also was an excellent amateur photographer. Untrained but insightful, he had been photographing favorite railroad subjects in the Milwaukee area, and as *Model Railroader* grew and he traveled for the magazine the young publisher began shooting around the country as well. And not just locomotives or action pictures. He was drawn to the atmospherics of railroading, its environment, its mark on the landscape, as well as the people who worked and rode on the trains. If his technical skill couldn't always match his ambitions, his photos still could be compelling.

Office legend has it that Al Kalmbach loved the railroad business even more than the model train hobby that gave him his start. If that's true, then the launching of *Trains* magazine in November 1940 was inevitable. Certainly it was an act of blind faith. Kalmbach could not count on industry support through advertising, and he wasn't interested in publishing a controlled-circulation trade paper in the manner of venerable *Railway Age*. Nor did he want to go the men's magazine route embodied by *Railroad*. Instead, he wanted to serve the nascent fraternity of railroad enthusiasts who shared a common preoccupation. They were already calling themselves "railfans."

It was obvious that photography would be a pillar of the new *Trains* even before the magazine was launched. In a special sixteen-page preview issued a month before the inaugural edition, Kalmbach promised a publication that would have "the unending curiosity of *National Geographic*." The reference to one of America's favorite magazines was not random. The famous yellow-framed *National Geographic* cover was a mainstay on living room coffee tables across the country, primarily because of the lavish pictures. The publisher emphatically put *Trains* in the same sort of company.

When the inaugural issue of *Trains* debuted a month later, Kalmbach reiterated the importance of pictures. The very first feature in the magazine's history wasn't about locomotives or railroad operations, but rather a keynote essay by Lucius Beebe, the *bon vivant* New York newspaper columnist widely credited with creating the railroad picture-book market in the late 1930s with a series of monographs for Appleton-Century and other publishers. The two-page spread in *Trains*, titled simply "Railroad Photography," included a handsome Beebe portrait of a Boston & Albany 4-6-4 on the point of New York Central's *New England States* rolling through suburban Boston.

Beebe delivered his message with typically overblown but stirring prose. "The satisfactions of action photography are all out of proportion to the effort, expense, and discouragements that may be encountered," Beebe famously wrote. "To stand poised at just the right angle and the right-hand side, to include the power reverse gear, with the sun over one's shoulder in the Cajon, listening to the thunder of exhaust of the helper and road engine of the *Chief* half a mile below, and know one has it, cold turkey, is one of the great delights of the business of living."

Beebe's insistence that the proper railroad photograph had to be made "just so" was destined to become an obsolete idea. Train pictures of that era remained a conservative affair, and Beebe was the genre's preeminent celebrity and tastemaker. The fact that he led off the first issue was everything the publisher needed to say about the place of photography in his fledgling magazine. At the end of the essay, Beebe even foreshadowed the eventual clout of his newest patron. "The shots will look fine, presumably blown up to 8 x 10 and carefully filed away, or it will be gratifying to see them reproduced with a credit line in *Trains*, but it's the getting them that counts."

TRAINS'S CLARION CALL GRADUALLY ATTRACTED a steady stream of submissions from a growing army of amateur photographers beginning to fan out across the country. It was a loose-knit fraternity dedicated at first to straight-ahead locomotive photography, often in the static, rods-down "roster" fashion achieved mostly inside engine terminals. The principal outlets for their work had been *Railroad* magazine—a poor prospect by any measure—as well as the simple act of selling or trading black-and-white prints and negatives at swap meets or by mail. The 35mm slide-show craze was still a decade or more off.

Security concerns with the onset of World War II brought most railroad photography to a relative standstill. Perhaps it was just as well; as the war dragged on, *Trains*, like all magazines, became subject to the rationing of raw materials, and for a time the publication was printed on cheap newsprint-grade paper. Photo reproduction suffered accordingly. Still, those first years helped show what was possible, and when the war ended the railfans were out again in force, now with an eye toward getting published in what had become the top publication in the field. Gradually, Kalmbach

Portrait of New York Central engineer John Hitchko in cab of 4-8-2 #3005, Galion, Ohio, September 1955. *Philip R. Hastings*

Lehigh Valley train #417 westbound at Hetcheltooth Curve, near Glen Onoko, Pennsylvania, October 1927. *Wayne Brumbaugh*

and his small staff got used to piles of mail coming in with reader submissions, covering every railroad in every corner of the United States and Canada.

The unforgiving demands of two monthly magazines quickly set the mold for Kalmbach's nascent archives. To feed their pages, the staffs of *Model Railroader* and *Trains* needed every kind of railroad picture imaginable. Readers were happy to oblige. In came roster shots of steam and diesel locomotives; action pictures of passenger and freight trains; scenes from roundhouses, freight yards, depot platforms, and interlocking towers. From the railroad public-relations departments came a flood of publicity photos of countless subjects: new steam and diesel locomotives; freight and passenger cars; staged scenes of fashionable models inside sleepers and lounge cars; grand openings of classification yards; railroad employees performing across all crafts; portraits of top executives. Similar pictures arrived from a supporting cast of suppliers, including locomotive builders such as Alco, Baldwin, Lima, and EMD; carbuilders like Pullman, Budd, and Thrall; and component manufacturers ranging from Westinghouse Air Brake and General Steel Castings to Timken and Union Switch and Signal.

With thousands of prints arriving throughout the year, some sort of organization was required. Without a full-time librarian or professional archivist, the editors directed most of the photos into file drawers arranged alphabetically by railroad, with separate

An engineman boards 2-8-2 #494,
Denver & Rio Grande Western,
Chama, New Mexico, 1961.
Richard Steinheimer

cabinets for suppliers. Some of the collections were small. Short lines, industrial railroads, and lumber companies didn't attract many photographers, so images of West Side Lumber, Sylvania Central, Mann's Creek, and their ilk often were kept in a single folder. The bigger railroads could require any number of subset files, moving front to back starting with locomotives and rolling stock through action photos to miscellaneous views of physical plant and people. Some of the categories could be huge, depending on the railroad. Union Pacific, for instance, required no fewer than twenty-six separate locomotive folders to cover everything from 0-4-0 switchers to 4-8-8-4 Big Boy articulateds and from NW2 diesel switchers to GE "Big Blow" gas turbines.

Collections of action pictures could become equally dense. Thanks to an explosion of interest where steam lingered in the late 1950s, a railroad such as the Nickel Plate or Norfolk & Western might quickly require a lot of file space. So many photographers shot latter-day steam on the N&W, for instance, that the railroad ended up with six separate steam action folders for Virginia alone. If an editor couldn't find the photo he wanted in "Steam Passenger: Radford Division," then maybe it would turn up in "Steam Passenger: Shenandoah Division" or "Steam Passenger: Norfolk Division." And distribution of files among the large Class I carriers was not proportional. With plenty of photographers nearby, railroads in the Northeast, the upper Midwest, and California were richly represented. There are thousands of pictures of New York Central, Baltimore & Ohio, Pennsylvania, and Santa Fe, for instance. Conversely, few *Trains* contributors worked in Texas or the Pacific Northwest, thus it's much more difficult to find the right photo if you need something on the Katy or the Great Northern.

Over the years, the archive also attracted images from photographers who had broken out from the railroad space and established reputations in the wider world of art photography. David Plowden, the renowned portraitist of the American landscape, has had a fruitful relationship with the magazine for a half century and proudly notes that his first published image (of Great Northern's *Empire Builder* near Glacier Park) appeared in *Trains* in December 1954. The files have also, at various times, contained numerous prints by O. Winston Link, the eccentric Madison Avenue photographer whose late-1950s depictions of fading Norfolk & Western steam dazzled the art world when his work was rediscovered in the 1980s and '90s. Other luminaries in the files include Fred Eidenbenz, a Swiss photographer drawn to U.S. railroading in the 1920s; Noel Hiram

Deeks, an assistant to the famed photographer and curator Edward Steichen; and Lewis Hine, the sociologist who in the early 1900s used his camera to advocate for social and labor reform.

ONE OF AL KALMBACH'S MYRIAD GIFTS was as a talent scout, and the group he assembled in the early years of *Trains* was something of a miracle. Looking back on the first fifteen years of the publication, it's astounding how many of the best published photos came not necessarily from far-flung freelancers but from Kalmbach's own employees, working out of the company's longtime headquarters at 1027 N. Seventh Street in downtown Milwaukee. These luminaries included the publisher himself, of course, but also Linn Westcott, W. A. "Bill" Akin Jr., and Wallace W. Abbey.

Westcott arrived at Kalmbach Publishing in 1935 and quickly proved to be the founder's right-hand man. He was incredibly versatile. A genius model railroader, Westcott was indispensable as a technical editor, electrical expert, cartographer, and track-plan designer, skills he would eventually bring to bear in his famous editorship of *Model Railroader* from 1961 to 1977. But Westcott was also a railroad enthusiast and a better than average photographer, especially when it came to recording physical plant, an outgrowth of his interest in modeling. Al Kalmbach even tapped his young editor to pair with Akin on a monthly column for *Trains* called simply "Railroad Photography," which ran in the late 1940s.

Akin and Abbey took Westcott one giant step better. First hired into the Kalmbach art department in 1947 and later named art director, Bill Akin proved to be an inventive photojournalist. The *Trains* staff made good use of Akin, sending him on a range of successful assignments that included riding the cab of a New York Central Niagara 4-8-4 on the *Empire State Express*, moving coal to tidewater on the Chesapeake & Ohio, and illustrating a major profile of the Chicago, Burlington & Quincy. Although Akin appears to have hung up his camera by the mid-1950s, when Kalmbach tapped him to run the company's press division, the Akin credit line accompanied some of the most daring photos of those early years.

And then there was Wally Abbey, the best staff photographer ever to grace the Kalmbach payroll. A talented journalist out of the University of Kansas, Abbey hired on to *Trains* as an associate editor in 1950 and quickly showed that he was the quintessential journalistic double threat, writing blockbuster feature stories often illustrated with his own blockbuster photographs. Abbey was a prime exponent of the new wave of railroad photography, deftly

depicting trains in their habitats and doing it as well as anybody. But he could also take intimate and highly evocative photos of the people of the railroad: lounge-car patrons caught in fleeting moments; redcaps and sleeping-car porters going about their unsung duties; conductors and engineers performing time-honored rituals at train time. Abbey's tenure was short—he left *Trains* in 1954 to pursue a successful railroad public relations career—but the crisp, vivid prints he left behind have remained a staple of the archives.

Abbey later said it was just good timing, but his departure for a railroad industry job coincided with the ascension to the editor's job of a friend, colleague, and, just possibly, a rival. But it didn't take long for everyone—readers, industry insiders, the publisher—to realize that *Trains* magazine was in brilliant hands. A growing legion of railroad photographers would know it too.

THE IMPACT OF DAVID P. MORGAN on railroad photography cannot be overstated. From the moment Al Kalmbach appointed him as editor of *Trains* in 1953, at the astoundingly young age of twenty-six, Morgan showed readers that the images in the magazine were not only going to be as important as the words, they would often be an entirely new kind of railroad picture. Morgan had dabbled in photography by that time, frequently making simple but competent shots of steam locomotives while he was hanging around stations and engine terminals, and he knew his limitations. A sign of his greatness, however, was that he knew when to put away the camera and instead nurture the talented contributors who could advance his vision.

A watershed moment came in November 1955 with the magazine's fifteenth anniversary issue. As if to coronate the new order, Morgan set aside an unprecedented fifteen pages for a special photo section to celebrate a dozen vanguard photographers. Each was afforded a single "favorite" photograph (most of them concerned with steam), and including a portrait of the photographer. The introduction was a mission statement for *Trains*'s approach to illustration. "The circulation and longevity of the magazine have been due in no mean measure to the photographers who've hauled their gear to trackside, there to record the ever-changing mode of the flanged wheel," Morgan wrote. "In a demanding yet specialized field of illustration the standards have been high and the material rewards necessarily meager."

Morgan correctly concluded that the pictures "are evidence that there is no ceiling on imaginative insight." Indeed, it was an all-star lineup that included William D. Middleton, Richard Steinheimer, Jim Shaughnessy, Wally Abbey, Philip R. Hastings, James A. LaVake, J. Parker Lamb, Robert Hale, Henry R. Griffiths, H. Reid, Don Sims, and Morgan's art director, Bill Akin. Most are represented in this book.

Three of them could be said to be paramount. If you thumb through the dog-eared prints in those old metal files, or leaf through three decades of pages in *Trains*, you'll marvel at how often you encounter credit lines for Hastings, Shaughnessy, and Steinheimer. They are considered by many to be the most significant of all the postwar photographers, and inarguably they were the most important to David P. Morgan. The latter fact alone confers upon them a singular status. Morgan adored their pictures, and along the way he made sure his readers had every opportunity to feel the same way. Not surprisingly, then, these three by far are most often represented in this volume. Much of that is a credit to their art, but some is due also to their ambition. All three were incredibly prolific, and although there's no question they did what they did because they loved it, they also knew they had a receptive market in their favorite editor from Milwaukee. They unabashedly wanted to get published—by Morgan.

MOST CLOSELY ASSOCIATED WITH THE EDITOR is Phil Hastings. From the moment his images arrived at *Trains* in 1946 the young photographer from New England grabbed the attention of the magazine's staff. Hastings didn't just take train pictures, or, least of all, locomotive pictures. Hastings was a pioneer in committing the entire railroad scene to film, sometimes in photographs filled with sprawling drama and action but also often in quiet, intimate moments. It was as if the photographer had found a way to synthesize all the elements of the railroad—geography, technology, the worker, commerce, the seasons, even history—into deceptively straightforward compositions.

It's fair to say that Hastings was Morgan's favorite collaborator. That much became obvious when the editor and the photographer decided to bring steam's last great act to the readers of *Trains*. It turned out to be a singular adventure in journalism. On separate journeys in 1954, '55, and '56, Morgan and Hastings climbed into the editor's Ford sedan to cover thousands of miles in eastern Canada, the northeastern United States, the upper Midwest, and the Appalachians, producing three landmark series for the magazine: "In Search of Steam" (1954), "Smoke Over the Prairies" (1955), and the magisterial "Steam in Indian Summer" (1956). Their accounts of diminutive 4-4-0s on branch lines in New Brunswick, giant Y6

Maine Central work train with 2-8-0 #516, St. Johnsbury, Vermont, September 1947. Philip R. Hastings

No. 4. Train No. 806 from Browns-
ville, Pa. No. 833 Northbound use
the same equipment. 7-27-46.
Note: No. 174 is a Mikado 2-8-2 Freight Locomotive. Yet it gave good service as a
passenger engine. No. 311 was in the shop.

No. 5. Engine No. 174 pinch hitting
for No. 311 while she is being in
the shop for repairs- 7-27-46.

No. 6. Crummy No. 32 with four
wheels Other have two 4 wheel

No. 7. Work Service Cars.
7- 27-46

Monon and Nickel Plate crossing,
Frankfort, Indiana, 1947.
Linn H. Westcott

Page from vintage photo album,
Monongahela Railway,
Fairmont, West Virginia, July 1946.
Roy Fidder

2-8-8-2s on Norfolk & Western's Blue Ridge, and fleet New York Central engines in Ohio and Illinois created a poignant you-are-there narrative that had readers waiting eagerly each month for the next installment.

Morgan's writing was already beginning to blossom before he made his trips with Hastings, and the steam safaris became a showcase for the mature, poetic prose that would sustain the editor for the rest of his thirty-three-year career at *Trains*. Goaded, perhaps, by his exposure to Morgan, Hastings responded with some of the best work of his career. These guys were in a hurry, so there is a true journalistic urgency to many of Hastings's images. But even in the most unexpected, chaotic moments he found a way to infuse his pictures with depth and *fin de siècle* heartbreak. Every image, every word is triumphantly bittersweet.

Evidence of the enduring appeal of their steam safaris is the fact that the entire series has been reprised twice: first as a hardcover book, *The Mohawk That Refused to Abdicate and Other Tales* (Kalmbach Books, 1975), and later as a series of three deluxe one-shot magazines from Kalmbach's *Classic Trains* quarterly in 2007, 2009, and 2011, edited by the photographer Greg McDonnell. Several images from the series are also part of this book.

IN JIM SHAUGHNESSY, MORGAN FOUND another kindred spirit, even though there is no evidence they traveled or directly worked together. Shaughnessy was another revolutionary practitioner. He told stories with his camera, immersing himself in all aspects of the railroad scene, refusing to rule out any photographic idea so long as it was practical. He was a lot like Hastings. In fact, the two photographers

Central Vermont way freight with 400-class 2-8-0 on winter morning, Bethel, Vermont, December 1956.
Jim Shaughnessy

were fellow travelers, figuratively and literally. They were close in age. They both were from the Northeast. They each received top-shelf educations that led to the professions, Hastings in psychiatry and Shaughnessy in civil engineering. Both were widely known to be self-effacing guys whose soft-spoken manners contrasted with the incredible ambition and work ethic that fed their photography. Friendly rivals, they traveled together on occasion, catching as much steam as they could in the upper Midwest, the Northeast, and especially eastern Canada.

Although he never got the marquee billing on the level of the steam safaris, Shaughnessy was all over the magazine. Beginning in the 1950s his images showed up in random feature stories, in countless editions of "Photo Section" (the magazine's regular gallery), in the "Railroad News Photos" department, and quite often paired with Morgan's prose in *Trains*'s signature frontispiece spreads. As time went on, Shaughnessy developed very good instincts about what the editor would want, and he exploited it. One of his rewards was magazine covers, and over the years Shaughnessy garnered thirteen of them, nearly a record among his compatriots. Hastings had twenty-five.

It's tempting to compare Hastings's and Shaughnessy's photographs and conclude they were working the same conceptual territory. And that's true, to some extent. Some of their images in this book look as if they were taken when the photographers were standing side by side. But where Hastings almost always touched an emotional nerve, to the point of sentiment, Shaughnessy's pictures have a more detached, analytical tone. Perhaps that's the difference between the viewpoint of a physician and an engineer. Certainly the distinctions were apparent in the prints that showed up in Morgan's inbox. Hastings did a good job in the darkroom, but it wasn't his strongest suit. His prints could be monochromatic, sometimes even grainy. Shaughnessy's, on the other hand, were brilliantly rendered, razor sharp except in the worst exterior conditions, with an excellent balance of tone and contrast. It's a safe bet that the compositors at the old Kalmbach Press had an easier time getting optimum halftones from Shaughnessy.

THOSE COMPOSITORS HAD NO SUCH TROUBLE with Richard Steinheimer, whose gorgeous prints began showing up in the Milwaukee office in 1948. A Southern Californian who got his start on his hometown Glendale *News-Press* after a stint in the Navy, Steinheimer was well qualified to chronicle the West. A tall, rangy, risk-taking outdoorsman, Steinheimer made muscular, adventurous, often cinematic portraits of trains working against the backdrops of mountain passes, bleak deserts, and the Pacific Ocean. In his early years he ranged widely over his home state, but he eventually went everywhere across the West. Like all of the magazine's first generation of photographers, he was initially drawn to steam; his work in this book centers on the Colorado narrow gauge.

In David Morgan, Steinheimer had the ideal audience. Morgan had grown up in Georgia and Kentucky, lived briefly in south Texas, and ended up working in Milwaukee, Wisconsin. Until his job at *Trains* afforded him the opportunity to travel frequently, for Morgan the West was a mythic place, more imagined by him than experienced. In Steinheimer, Morgan saw a kind of John Ford of railroad photography, someone who was from the West, of the West, and eager to show it off to anyone hailing from east of Salt Lake City. *Trains* was aiming for a truly national readership, and the West—especially California—grabbed the imagination of everybody, no matter where they called home.

The West produced a number of top-shelf photographers, notably represented in this volume by Robert Hale, Stan Kistler, and Richard H. "Dick" Kindig. But Steinheimer was the one Morgan would call upon again and again. An office wag—himself a Steinheimer admirer—has noted that Morgan seemed especially susceptible to the photographer on account of the oversize, gallery-suitable prints that arrived in his fifth-floor office from California. No doubt they were knockouts as they emerged from their boxes. What editor wouldn't be impressed, even seduced?

In 1961 Kalmbach Books confirmed Steinheimer's master status with the release of *Backwoods Railroads of the West,* a high-end, gravure-printed showcase of black-and-white photography replete with steam railroading. As Morgan wrote in the introduction, Steinheimer is "that passing rare triumvirate: a photographic technician, a man knowledgeable in the ways of railroading, someone talented to the degree of becoming an artist … he is fearfully authentic, too much so for comfort upon occasion … Dick Steinheimer consistently exhausts my feelings."

Perhaps more than his fellow first-generation stars, Steinheimer adapted easily as railroading changed. The loss of steam had hung over that November 1955 photo essay, but Steinheimer's contribution was a triptych of a Southern Pacific piggyback train hauled by F7 diesels. Bucking the general sentiment of the photo story, the photographer commented that "I somehow can't feel that dieselization

and growth of the industry are a disaster." He would prove it over the ensuing three decades with an unequaled string of cover-story photo essays dedicated to such iconic themes as Cajon Pass, Donner Pass, the Tehachapi Mountains, and the Milwaukee Road in Montana and Idaho. Quite an accomplishment for a man who, in the 1955 showcase, had described himself to Morgan as "just a rail photo bum."

STEINHEIMER'S EASY *RAPPROCHEMENT* with the diesel mirrored the editor's own. Of all of Morgan's accomplishments during his thirty-three-year reign as editor, perhaps the greatest—at least insofar as the magazine's longevity as a business was concerned—was his ability to get his readers to fall in love with the diesel. The demise of steam had threatened *Trains* in the early '50s as thousands of brokenhearted iron horse devotees fell away. But from the mid-1950s onward Morgan found fresh ways to make railroading vivid and exciting, and his central thrust was to celebrate the internal-combustion locomotive on its own terms.

That was good for the magazine, and certainly good for its mission as a journal of railroad photography. New generations of inventive photographers bought in to what Morgan was saying and continued to go trackside, inspired to wring as much drama as possible out of railroading's new order of hood units, intermodal trains, welded rail, and CTC operations. It's quite possible that in the years after 1960 the archive added more photos than it ever saw in the steam era. The collection grew in stature as well: Hastings, Steinheimer, and the rest of their cohort inspired a second generation of trailblazing photographers, most of them using 35mm SLR cameras and telephoto lenses and working in the 35mm color slide format.

In its second quarter century, the *Trains* photo archive continued to flourish. One reason was the arrival of George H. Drury in 1972. He was hired at first to help edit books, but Morgan gradually moved him into the library after devising a way to make the librarian job a shared, part-time position. Although a competent photographer, Drury had no significant role in advancing the content of the photo archive. Yet he quickly became the collection's dedicated custodian, first in the company's longtime office in downtown Milwaukee and, after 1988, at its new headquarters in suburban Waukesha. Drury intelligently reorganized many of the photo files, making them easier for editors to navigate, and he created new categories to accommodate images that didn't fit the usual assumptions. He applied a modest discipline on editors who got too sloppy with the

assets. And he made the library a pleasant place to work, usually with classical music in the background, always with fresh flowers on the study table.

Morgan's editorship—and his stewardship of the archive—would last until his unexpected retirement in 1987 (followed by his untimely death in 1990 at age sixty-two). It would be up to other *Trains* editors to sustain the magazine's photographic mission amid big changes in photography. By the late 1980s, as the flow of incoming black-and-white pictures slowed to a trickle, the library added a modest filing system for 35mm slides, although it never came close to matching the original print collection.

Bigger numbers came in the new millennium as nearly all of *Trains*'s contributors switched to digital cameras. This time, a third generation of young photographers came of age who sent in their images via e-mail and DVD, obliging the editors and designers to learn an entirely new system characterized by RAW files, JPEG images, and other expressions of the pixilated railroad photo. The magazine reached a landmark of a sort in the late summer of 2014 when its editors estimated they had committed a total of 100,000 digital images to today's "archive," actually a bank of data servers maintained by Kalmbach's Information Services department.

Today's *Trains* relies almost exclusively on a system of digital image management for coverage of contemporary railroading, which remains the magazine's essential mission. The editors occasionally tap into the old archive across the hall, but the library is much quieter, and the banks of file cabinets are more the province of the staffs of *Classic Trains, Model Railroader*, and, occasionally, a visiting author or researcher. What hasn't changed is the company's commitment to the archive. The photographic vision of founder Al Kalmbach and David P. Morgan and their inheritors remains intact. Today's *Trains* editors might work in a digital world characterized by passwords and metadata, but they can always walk through those library doors and experience the spiritual and tactile satisfaction of holding up to the light all those thousands of priceless 5 x 7 and 8 x 10 silver-gelatin prints, their backs scrawled with the handwritten captions and rubber-stamped credit lines of three generations of trailblazing photographers who answered the magazine's call.

Kevin P. Keefe is vice president–editorial at Kalmbach Publishing Co., and a former editor and publisher of Trains.

Norfolk & Western Y6-class 2-8-8-2s, Grundy, Virginia, March 26, 1959.
Bruce R. Meyer

Photographs

PLATE 1 Northern Alberta
Railways trains, Busby, Alberta,
October 25, 1952. *Donald E. Smith*

PLATE 2 Baltimore & Ohio 2-8-2 #4443 at Lumberton, West Virginia, 1955. *James P. Gallagher*

PLATE 3 Baltimore & Ohio helper engines, Amblersburg, West Virginia, March 20, 1948. *Charles A. Brown*

PLATE 4 Pennsylvania Railroad 4-8-2 #6921, Northumberland, Pennsylvania, 1956. *Don Wood*

PLATE 5 East Broad Top Railroad 2-8-2 #14, at Orbisonia, Pennsylvania, July 10, 1952. *Philip R. Hastings*

PLATE 6 Canadian Pacific 2-8-2s, Cookshire, Quebec, 1956.
Jim Shaughnessy

PLATE 7 Charleston & Western Carolina 2-8-0 #823, Augusta, Georgia, July 1944.
Alex L. H. Darragh

PLATE 8 E&G Brooke 0-4-0 #3,
Birdsboro, Pennsylvania, September 27, 1957.
Aaron G. Fryer

PLATE 9 Boston & Maine 2-10-2 #2902, Woodsville, New Hampshire, April 1947. *Philip R. Hastings*

PLATE 10 Illinois Central's *Hawkeye* at Waterloo, Iowa, mid-1950s. *Philip R. Hastings*

PLATE 11 Union Pacific freight train,
Snake River Valley, Idaho, October 17, 1953.
David W. Salter

PLATE 12 Baird Creek Trestle,
southwest Washington, 1940.
Weyerhaeuser Company

PLATE 13 Union Lumber Company,
Fort Bragg, California, date unknown.
Wonacott's Studio

PLATE 14 Denver & Rio Grande Western 2-8-2,
Durango, Colorado, 1961.
Richard Steinheimer

PLATE 15 Canadian National 4-8-4 #6179,
Rivière-du-Loup, Quebec, 1953.
Philip R. Hastings

PLATE 16 Denver & Rio Grande Western 4-6-6-4 #3702, Kyune, Utah, date unknown. *R. H. Kindig*

PLATE 17 Norfolk & Western 2-8-8-2, Narrows, Virginia, 1954. W. A. Akin Jr.

previous spread:

PLATE 18 Pennsylvania Railroad's
Broad Street Station, Philadelphia, 1923.
Pennsylvania Railroad

PLATE 19 Denver & Rio Grande Western #499,
Toltec Siding, Colorado, 1956.
Philip R. Hastings

PLATE 20 Long Island Rail Road terminal, Morris Park, New York, 1942–'45. *Long Island Rail Road*

PLATE 21 Pennsylvania Railroad 4-6-2 #5471, South Amboy, New Jersey, May 1956. *Don Wood*

PLATE 22 Norfolk & Western 4-8-4,
near Roanoke, Virginia, 1956.
Robert Hale

PLATE 23 Denver, Northwestern & Pacific 4-6-2 #100
near Phantom Bridge, Corona, Colorado, 1910. *L. C. McClure*

PLATE 24 Union Pacific construction
near Dale Creek, Wyoming, 1868. *A. J. Russell*

No 634 Miller & Pattersons Cut No 2 East of Nevada

previous spread:

PLATE 28 Boston & Maine 4-6-2,
Boston North Station, November 1947.
Philip R. Hastings

PLATE 29 Long Island Rail Road,
Morris Park terminal, date unknown.
Long Island Rail Road

PLATE 30 Canadian National 4-8-2 #6000,
Pointe St. Charles Shops, Montreal, 1923.
Cecil Fray collection

PLATE 31 Denver & Rio Grande Western 2-8-2 #478, Durango, Colorado, January 1961.
Richard Steinheimer

PLATE 32 Chicago, Burlington & Quincy 2-10-2s, Edgemont, South Dakota, 1948.
G. B. Taylor

PLATE 33 Louisville & Nashville engine terminal, Hazard, Kentucky, 1948.
Louisville & Nashville

PLATE 34 Chicago & North Western 4-6-2s, Chicago, Illinois, August 24, 1953.
Wallace W. Abbey

PLATE 35 Union Pacific 4-6-6-4 #3832, eastern Wyoming, 1956. *Robert Hale*

PLATE 36 Union Pacific mixed train,
near Smith's Ferry, Idaho, December 31, 1947.
R. H. Kindig

PLATE 37 Pennsylvania Railroad 4-8-2 #6761, Harrisburg, Pennsylvania, March 4, 1956. *Don Wood*

PLATE 38 Nickel Plate Road 2-8-4 #814 with fireman filling tender, Cleveland, Ohio, 1958. *Art Hanford*

PLATE 39 Canadian National 4-8-4 #6234 in roundhouse, Hamilton, Ontario, December 1958. *Philip R. Hastings*

PLATE 40 Chicago & North Western depot, Barrington, Illinois, March 1941. *Bill Rusk*

PLATE 41 Central Vermont 2-10-4 #703,
Roxbury, Vermont, 1954–'55. *Paul A. Reynolds*

PLATE 42 Canadian Pacific 1200-class 4-6-2,
Ottawa, Ontario, January 1955. *D. L. McQueen*

PLATE 43 Canadian National 4-8-4 #6167,
Toronto, Ontario, May 20, 1962.
Robert Gilmour

PLATE 44 Union Pacific "Big Boy" engineer,
east of Laramie, Wyoming, 1956.
Robert Hale

PLATE 45 Texas & Pacific station,
Denton, Texas, September 21, 1941.
Charles M. Mizell Jr.

78

PLATE 47 Duluth & Northeastern 2-8-0 #16,
Cloquet, Minnesota, August 7, 1961.
Philip R. Hastings

PLATE 48 Pennsylvania Railroad 4-4-2 #759, Philadelphia, May 22, 1937. *E. Stanley Hart Jr.*

PLATE 49 Baltimore & Ohio 4-6-2 #5300, Baltimore, Maryland, January 1952. *James P. Gallagher*

PLATE 50 Santa Fe 4-4-2 #1440, south of Denver, Colorado, 1910. *L. C. McClure*

PLATE 51 Erie Railroad, Starrucca Viaduct, Lanesboro, Pennsylvania, date unknown. *Erie Railroad*

PLATE 52 Illinois Central flooding at Memphis, Tennessee, April 1912. *Illinois Central*

NEAR HELM, MISS.
BR. L 132-6
5-9-27

PLATE 53 Illinois Central flooding at Helm, Mississippi, May 9, 1927. *Illinois Central*

PLATE 54 Illinois Central engine terminal, Centralia, Illinois, August 1, 1912. *Illinois Central*

PLATE 55 Baltimore & Ohio, Bollman truss bridge, Harpers Ferry, West Virginia, date unknown. *B&O Railroad*

PLATE 56 Oneida & Western 2-8-0 #28,
northeastern Tennessee, 1954.
Philip R. Hastings

PLATE 57 Canadian National 4-6-0 #1576, at Palmerston, Ontario, February 1958.
Jim Shaughnessy

PLATE 58 Duluth & Northeastern 2-8-0 #27, Cloquet, Minnesota, January 1962.
John Gruber

PLATE 59 Santa Fe 4-8-4 #3781,
Canyon Diablo, Arizona, 1947.
Santa Fe Railway

PLATE 60 Central Railroad of New Jersey,
Terminal semaphore signals,
Jersey City, New Jersey, 1967.
David Plowden

PLATE 61 Illinois Central 0-8-0 #3541, Champaign, Illinois, November 30, 1958. *Ed Wojtas*

PLATE 62 Norfolk & Western 4-8-2 #104, Bristol, Virginia, 1957. O. Winston Link

PLATE 63 New York Central 4-6-4 #5249, Harmon, New York, 1949. *Ed Nowak*

PLATE 64 Terminal interlocking tower, 1944. *Union Switch & Signal*

PLATE 65 Canadian National 4-6-4,
Oakville, Ontario, February 15, 1958.
Jim Shaughnessy

previous spread:

PLATE 66 Southern Pacific track worker,
San Francisco, California, 1950.
Richard Steinheimer

PLATE 67 Central Railroad of New Jersey bridge,
Lehighton, Pennsylvania, 1965.
David Plowden

PLATE 68 Rock Island 4-8-2,
Clinton, Oklahoma, late 1940s.
Joe Conn

PLATE 69 Southern Railway 4-8-2, Dendron, North Carolina, 1944. *Frank Clodfelter*

PLATE 70 Graham County Railroad Shay #1926, Nantahala Gorge, North Carolina, September 1962. *J. E. Bradley*

PLATE 71 Central Railroad of New Jersey, Jersey City Terminal, May 18, 1953.
Philip R. Hastings

PLATE 72 Pennsylvania Railroad station, Harrisburg, Pennsylvania, April 1948.
Linn H. Westcott

PLATE 73 - 84 Vignettes from the Lehigh Valley Railroad and the New Haven Railroad, 1941–'42. *Noel Hiram Deeks*

PLATE 85 Virginia & Truckee 4-6-0 #27,
Steamboat Springs, Nevada, 1948.
Lucius Beebe

PLATE 86 Baltimore & Ohio 2-8-2 #4493, near Dayton, Ohio, January 1956.
J. Parker Lamb

PLATE 87 Northern Pacific 4-8-4, Bozeman, Montana, February 13, 1941.
E. R. Augustin Jr.

PLATE 88 Southern Pacific shops, Sacramento, California, 1941. *Southern Pacific*

PLATE 89 Canadian National 0-8-0 #8421,
Toronto, Ontario, July 4, 1958.
Bruce R. Meyer

PLATE 90 Southern Pacific 4-8-8-2
at Saugus, California, 1952.
M. M. Deaderick

PLATE 91 Canadian National
4-8-4, London, Ontario, late 1930s.
Canadian National

PLATE 92 Pennsylvania Railroad
4-6-2 #830, South Amboy,
New Jersey, January 1, 1957.
Don Wood

PLATE 93 Canadian National 4-6-2 #5288
near Sherbrooke, Quebec, February 1957.
Jim Shaughnessy

PLATE 94 Norfolk & Western 4-8-2,
Hagerstown, Maryland, March 1956.
O. Winston Link

PLATE 95 Pennsylvania-Reading
Seashore Lines 4-4-2 #6085,
Camden, New Jersey, 1949.
John Fulginiti

PLATE 96 Chicago & North Western E-class 4-6-2, Milwaukee, Wisconsin, 1940. *Linn H. Westcott*

PLATE 97 Washing Nickel Plate Road 2-8-2, Frankfort, Indiana, 1943. *William M. Rittase*

PLATE 98 New York Central engine
terminal, Harmon, New York, 1920s.
Fred Eidenbenz

PLATE 99 New York Central engine terminal
and coaling station, Rensselaer, New York, 1930s.
New York Central

PLATE 100 Denver, Northwestern & Pacific train, above Plainview, Colorado, early 1900s. *H. H. Buckwalter collection, Ph.00057, History Colorado*

PLATE 101 Central Vermont 2-8-0, at Rouses Point, New York, 1955. *Jim Shaughnessy*

PLATE 102 Canadian National station, Niagara Falls, Ontario, August 24, 1953. *Wallace W. Abbey*

PLATE 103 Chicago, Burlington & Quincy station stop, McCook, Nebraska, 1948. *Philip Morris, for Bendix Radio*

PLATE 104 Denver & Rio Grande Western, Durango, Colorado, January 30, 1961. *Richard Steinheimer*

PLATE 105 East Broad Top roundhouse, Orbisonia, Pennsylvania, July 10, 1952. *Philip R. Hastings*

137

PLATE 106 Norfolk & Western Y6-class 2-8-8-2s, Iaeger, West Virginia, March 26, 1959. Bruce R. Meyer

PLATE 107 Canadian Pacific 2-8-0 #3554, Chipman, New Brunswick, October 1953. *Philip R. Hastings*

PLATE 108 Canadian Pacific 2-8-2 #5214, Bayview Junction, Ontario, January 28, 1959. *Frank Barry*

PLATE 109 Southern Railway 4-6-2 #1407, Lynchburg, Virginia, May 1950. *H. Reid*

PLATE 110 Baltimore & Ohio EM-1
2-8-8-4 #7605 at Painesville, Ohio, 1955.
Jim Shaughnessy

PLATE 111 Chesapeake & Ohio 2-6-6-6 #1624, Thurmond, West Virginia, 1955. *Philip R. Hastings*

PLATE 112 Rock Island passenger train at Sheffield, Illinois, August 2, 1911. *Roy Campbell collection*

PLATE 113 Louisville & Nashville 4-6-2,
Venedy, Illinois, 1953. *Warren Stricker*

PLATE 114 Boston & Maine 4-6-2 #3623,
White River Junction, Vermont, late 1940s.
Philip R. Hastings

PLATE 115 Canadian National
Continental Limited at Saskatoon,
Saskatchewan, 1952. W. A. Akin Jr.

PLATE 116 Baltimore & Ohio switchers,
Brunswick, Maryland, September 1953.
James P. Gallagher

following spread:

PLATE 117 Central Vermont 2-8-0 #501,
Brattleboro, Vermont, 1956.
Jim Shaughnessy

PLATE 118 Southern Pacific engineer,
Mojave, California, 1948.
Ward Kimball

PLATE 119 Norfolk & Western terminal, Norfolk, Virginia, January 1957.
Mallory Hope Ferrell

PLATE 120 New York Central 4-8-2 #3005, Galion, Ohio, September 1955.
Philip R. Hastings

PLATE 121 New York Central 4-6-4- #5403, Mattoon, Illinois, September 1954.
Philip R. Hastings

PLATE 122 Canadian National
caboose interior, New Brunswick, 1955.
Philip R. Hastings

PLATE 123 Union Pacific 4-8-8-4 #4009, Dale Junction, Wyoming, August 20, 1957. *Jim Shaughnessy*

PLATE 124 Maine Central mixed train at Crawford Notch, New Hampshire, 1952. *Frank Clodfelter*

PLATE 125 Southern Railway 2-8-2 #4505,
Saluda Grade, North Carolina, August 3, 1950.
August A. Thieme Jr.

following spread:

PLATE 126 Canadian National 4-8-4 #6147,
London, Ontario, late 1930s.
Canadian National Railway

PLATE 127 Illinois Central 2-8-2,
Cairo, Illinois, 1950.
Henry J. McCord

PLATE 128 Wabash Railroad 4-4-0 #659,
Chicago, Illinois, June 12, 1931.
A. W. Johnson

PLATE 129 Chicago & North Western
4-6-2 #2901, Madison, Wisconsin,
July 9, 1955. *William D. Middleton*

PLATE 130 Southern Pacific cabooses,
Roseville Yard, California, 1958.
Philip R. Hastings

PLATE 131 Rock Island station at Decorah, Iowa, 1950s. *Philip R. Hastings*

PLATE 132 Southern Pacific 4-8-8-2 #4165, Colton, California, 1951. *Richard Steinheimer*

PLATE 133 Denver & Rio Grande Western 2-8-2 #483, Cumbres Pass, Colorado, early 1960s. *Richard Steinheimer*

PLATE 134 Baltimore & Ohio yards, Buckhannon, West Virginia, 1949. *H. Reid*

PLATE 135 Canadian Pacific 4-6-4 #2838, London, Ontario, August 1959. *Ted Rose*

PLATE 136 Maine Central 4-6-0 #371, Crawford Notch, New Hampshire, October 1952. *Philip R. Hastings*

PLATE 137 Georgia-Pacific Shay #19, Log Cabin, West Virginia, date unknown. *W. G. Gordon*

PLATE 138 Canadian Pacific 4-6-2 #2457, Sherbrooke, Quebec, November 1953. *Philip R. Hastings*

PLATE 139 Wichita Falls & Southern 2-8-0 #30, Ranger, Texas, 1945. *Lucius Beebe*

Captions

Plate 1 Northern Alberta Railways trains, Busby, Alberta, October 25, 1952. *Donald E. Smith*

Two Northern Alberta Railways trains meet at Busby, Alberta, 40 miles north of Edmonton, at the junction of NAR's main line and its Barrhead Branch, on October 25, 1952. At left is train 26, the Tuesday-Thursday-Saturday mixed train from Barrhead, led by 2-8-0 #74. Taking on water is 2-10-0 #53 on the head end of an extra freight from McLennon.

Plate 2 Baltimore & Ohio 2-8-2 #4443 at Lumberton, West Virginia, 1955. *James P. Gallagher*

A Baltimore & Ohio 2-8-2 #4443 pulls an eastbound coal train across Ten Mile Creek and past the yard at Lumberton, West Virginia, where the local switcher is working. The train in this 1955 photo originated in New Martinsville, on the Ohio River, and is headed for Fairmont along B&O's Monongah Division in the north-central part of the Mountain State.

Plate 3 Baltimore & Ohio helper engines, Amblersburg, West Virginia, March 20, 1948. *Charles A. Brown*

A pair of helper Mallet locomotives—a 2-8-8-0 and an 0-8-8-0—push on the bay-window caboose at the rear of a 54-car Baltimore & Ohio coal drag climbing past Amblersburg, West Virginia, on March 20, 1948. The train is eastbound, headed for Terra Alta along the mountainous Cumberland Division's tortuous 12-mile Cranberry Grade.

Plate 4 Pennsylvania Railroad 4-8-2 #6921, Northumberland, Pennsylvania, 1956. *Don Wood*

A hostler at the Pennsylvania Railroad's roundhouse in Northumberland, Pennsylvania, wipes down the cylinder-head cover of M1 4-8-2 #6921 as it takes a break between assignments in 1956. A 2-8-0 also is being kept under steam in the adjacent stall. Northumberland was one of the last bastions of PRR steam before the railroad completely dieselized in 1957.

Plate 5 East Broad Top Railroad 2-8-2 #14, at Orbisonia, Pennsylvania, July 10, 1952. *Philip R. Hastings*

Pennsylvania's famed narrow-gauge East Broad Top Railroad & Coal Company is still hanging on to its coal-hauling business on a July night in 1952 as 2-8-2 #14 rides the turntable at the EBT roundhouse in Orbisonia. Located in the south-central part of the state and connecting with the Pennsylvania Railroad at Mount Union, the company would end its coal business in 1956. Baldwin built the Mikado in 1914.

Plate 6 Canadian Pacific 2-8-2s, Cookshire, Quebec, 1956. *Jim Shaughnessy*

Double-headed steam locomotives are still commonplace on the Canadian Pacific's New Brunswick District in the winter of 1956 as a freight train pauses for servicing at Cookshire, Quebec, behind a pair of P-class 2-8-2s. The fireman is taking on water on the lead engine for the remainder of the run to Lac-Mégantic, 47 miles to the east.

Plate 7 Charleston & Western Carolina 2-8-0 #823, Augusta, Georgia, July 1944. *Alex L. H. Darragh*

The engine crew of Charleston & Western Carolina 2-8-0 #823 puts their shoulders into an "armstrong" manual turntable at the regional line's yard in Augusta, Georgia, in July 1944. The C&WC operated 341 miles of railroad in Georgia and South Carolina until absorbed by parent Atlantic Coast Line in 1959.

Plate 8 E&G Brooke 0-4-0 #3, Birdsboro, Pennsylvania, September 27, 1957. *Aaron G. Fryer*

A crewman cleans the fire of 0-4-0 #3 against a backdrop of smoke and steam from the E&G Brooke iron mill and furnaces in Birdsboro, Pennsylvania, near Reading, on September 27, 1957. The saddletank engine was built by Alco-Cooke in 1910 and served at this plant after 1925. By the time of the photograph the entire facility was a subsidiary of Colorado Fuel & Iron.

Plate 9 Boston & Maine 2-10-2 #2902, Woodsville, New Hampshire, April 1947. *Philip R. Hastings*

Yard floodlights illuminate the water column at Woodsville, New Hampshire, as Boston & Maine 2-10-2 #2902 on symbol freight D-J-2 pauses for water in April 1947. The time exposure for a night photograph was a necessity: by this time, the S-class Texas-types operated only at night on this and corresponding trains between Berlin, New Hampshire, and White River Junction, Vermont.

Plate 10 Illinois Central's *Hawkeye* at Waterloo, Iowa, mid-1950s. *Philip R. Hastings*

A postal clerk looks down pensively from the open door of a combination railway post office–baggage car as Illinois Central's train 12, the *Hawkeye*, the overnight train from Sioux City to Chicago, pauses just after midnight in Waterloo for servicing in April 1967. Waterloo was the halfway point in the train's 510-mile journey. Later in the same year, the Post Office Department would eliminate most RPO service, including the *Hawkeye's*.

Plate 11 Union Pacific freight train, Snake River Valley, Idaho, October 17, 1953.
David W. Salter

Two articulated steam locomotives have been summoned to haul a westbound Union Pacific freight up the long grade out of the Snake River valley east of Reverse, Idaho, on the morning of October 17, 1953. On the front of the train is 4-6-6-4 Challenger #3985, destined to have a second life in the 1980s as a UP excursion engine. At the rear is a pusher, 2-8-8-0 #3528.

Plate 12 Baird Creek Trestle, southwest Washington, 1940.
Weyerhaeuser Company

A narrow-gauge steam locomotive slowly pushes a work train across the 1,130-foot-long Baird Creek Trestle during the bridge's construction in 1940 at Weyerhaeuser Company's sprawling St. Helens Tree Farm in southwestern Washington near Longview. The trestle towered 235 feet above the creek and was dismantled in 1961 when the timber company closed the railroad.

Plate 13 Union Lumber Company, Fort Bragg, California. *Wonacott's Studio*

Redwood logs ride the flatcars of the California Western Railroad & Navigation Company at the Union Lumber Company sawmill in coastal Fort Bragg, California, in an early-twentieth-century photograph. The 40-mile railroad hauled logs to the mill and finished lumber east to Willits for interchange with the Northwestern Pacific. Portions of the railroad survive today as the California Western.

Plate 14 Denver & Rio Grande Western 2-8-2, Durango, Colorado, 1961.
Richard Steinheimer

Double-headed narrow-gauge 2-8-2s have just come in off a freight train at dusk at Denver & Rio Grande Western's roundhouse in Durango, Colorado, in 1961. Working by torchlight, the engine crew walks around the locomotives to drain air tanks, check bearing temperatures, grease the rods, and open cylinder cocks before the engines are put away for the night.

Plate 15 Canadian National 4-8-4 #6179, Rivière-du-Loup, Quebec, 1953.
Philip R. Hastings

With the engineer and fireman looking on, a ground crew works on a balky steam line between engine and tender as Canadian National 4-8-4 #6179 pauses in Rivière-du-Loup, Quebec, with the Halifax-Montreal *Maritime Express* in late 1953. Montreal Locomotive Works delivered the dual-service Northern in 1940.

Plate 16 Denver & Rio Grande Western 4-6-6-4 #3702, Kyune, Utah.
R. H. Kindig

Denver & Rio Grande Western 4-6-6-4 #3702 blasts a column of coal smoke skyward as it climbs Soldier Summit grade through the Price River Valley near Kyune, Utah, with a 47-car westbound train. Even with two more locomotives pushing on the rear, their exhaust visible in the distance around the curve, the train is down to a 10-mph crawl up the nearly 2.4 percent grade.

Plate 17 Norfolk & Western 2-8-8-2, Narrows, Virginia, 1954.
W. A. Akin Jr.

Glimpsed from U.S. Highway 460 across the New River Valley, one of Norfolk & Western's giant homebuilt Y6-class 2-8-8-2s drifts downgrade at Narrows, Virginia, with an eastbound freight train in the summer of 1954. Steam still rules on this busy section of N&W's Radford Division between the company's headquarters in Roanoke, Virginia, and the division point of Bluefield, West Virginia.

Plate 18 Pennsylvania Railroad's Broad Street Station, Philadelphia, 1923.
Pennsylvania Railroad

The denuded steel frame of the Pennsylvania Railroad's train shed at Philadelphia's Broad Street Station looms over workmen building new wooden platforms in the aftermath of the huge June 11, 1923, fire that destroyed much of the station. MP54 MU electric commuter trains are parked at left and steam locomotives dominate on the right. The station would close permanently in April 1952.

Plate 19 Denver & Rio Grande Western #499, Toltec Siding, Colorado, 1956.
Philip R. Hastings

The headlight of Denver & Rio Grande Western narrow-gauge 2-8-2 #499 peers into the freezing darkness as it waits at Toltec Siding with 51 cars to meet an oncoming train in 1956. Even in spring, heavy snow can be expected at this point along the D&RGW's extension through the San Juan Mountains. The elevation at this location on the railroad is in excess of 9,400 feet.

Plate 20 Long Island Rail Road terminal, Morris Park, New York, 1942–'45. *Long Island Rail Road*

At the height of World War II men and women work together on the American railroad, here at the Long Island Rail Road's Morris Park engine house near Jamaica, Queens, as machinist helpers Ann Douglas Mason and John Crawford grease the driving rods and 80-inch driving wheels of a K4s 4-6-2 of LIRR owner Pennsylvania Railroad.

Plate 21 Pennsylvania Railroad 4-6-2 #5471, South Amboy, New Jersey, May 1956.
Don Wood

An engineer on the Pennsylvania Railroad's New York Region extra board climbs aboard #5471, one of PRR's famed K4s Pacifics, at South Amboy, New Jersey, in May 1956. Soon, he and his 4-6-2 will take the reins from an electric locomotive on train 787, a Sunday-only commuter train from New York's Penn Station headed down the New Jersey coast on the New York & Long Branch Division, one of the last strongholds for steam on the PRR.

Plate 22 Norfolk & Western 4-8-4, near Roanoke, Virginia, 1956.
Robert Hale

Photographed at speed from an adjacent highway in 1956, a Norfolk & Western J-class 4-8-4 rolls along the main line with a passenger train near Roanoke, Virginia. N&W built 14 of the unusually powerful Northern-type engines, 3 of them in 1950, all at the company's Roanoke Shops. With their streamlining, their high-pressure boilers, and roller bearings on lightweight driving rods, these fast engines defined the pinnacle in steam locomotive design, hauling such premier N&W trains as the *Pocahontas* and the *Powhatan Arrow*.

Plate 23 Denver, Northwestern & Pacific 4-6-2 #100 near Phantom Bridge, Corona, Colorado, 1910.
L. C. McClure

High in the Rockies, a distinguished crowd has detrained from a Denver, Northwestern & Pacific special passenger train on the 23-mile route over Rollins Pass in the Front Range above Denver. Financier David Moffat began building the railroad in 1902 to offer his city a direct railroad route to the west. His tortuous main line over the Front Range came to be called the "Giant's Ladder" and ultimately included 33 tunnels and reached its highest elevation at 11,680 feet until made obsolete with the 1928 opening of the 6.2-mile-long Moffat Tunnel.

Plate 24 Union Pacific construction near Dale Creek, Wyoming, 1868.
A. J. Russell

Workers pause in Cut No. 6, known as Miller and Patterson's Cut, as they build the Union Pacific westward near Dale Creek in southeast Wyoming. The photograph was made less than a year before UP's rendezvous with the eastward-building Central Pacific at Promontory, Utah, on May 10, 1869. Russell launched his career during the Civil War as the Union Army's first official photographer with the U.S. Military Railroad, after which he famously documented the transcontinental railroad. His album *The Great West Illustrated* was a bestseller when published by UP in 1869.

Plate 25 Norfolk & Western 4-8-4s, Cincinnati Union Terminal, September 1952.
Wallace W. Abbey

Norfolk & Western train No. 3, the *Pocahontas*, has arrived at Cincinnati Union Terminal on a September 1952 morning after its 667-mile overnight run from Norfolk, Virginia, via Roanoke, Virginia, and Portsmouth, Ohio. One of the train's two sleeping cars will continue to Chicago on a Pennsylvania Railroad train. On the head end of the *Pocahontas* are two of N&W's streamlined J-class 4-8-4s, famous for their ability to use their relatively small 70-inch driving wheels to develop both speed and power across the mountainous Pocahontas Division in West Virginia. Both locomotives were built by the railroad at its Roanoke Shops.

Plate 26 Nickel Plate Road 2-8-4 #814, with engineer inside cab, near Ashtabula, Ohio, 1958.
Art Hanford

Nickel Plate Road engineer Walter L. Herbel, a homemade cigarette dangling from his lips, has his gloved left hand on the grapevine throttle and his right hand on the whistle cord of 2-8-4 # 814, a former Wheeling & Lake Erie engine, making 50 mph down the NKP main line out of Bellevue, Ohio, in the spring of 1958 with eastbound train CC-2 for Conneaut, Ohio. The photographer made the images for a story in the Brotherhood of Locomotive Engineers' member publication *The Locomotive Engineer*.

Plate 27 Santa Fe freight train, Tehachapi Mountains, California, December 1952.
Stan Kistler

On December 14, 1952, Santa Fe freight train Extra 225 West slowly squeals around a 15-degree curve on a shoofly track constructed around a collapsed tunnel, just five months after the July 21, 1952, earthquake that severely damaged Southern Pacific's main line, shared with Santa Fe through the Tehachapi Mountains of Southern California between Mojave and Bakersfield. Losses from the quake were estimated at $60 million. It took SP 25 days to reopen the railroad.

Plate 28 Boston & Maine 4-6-2, Boston North Station, November 1947.
Philip R. Hastings

An early-morning local train on the Boston & Maine's Portland Division departs Boston's North Station, accelerating past lines of commuter coaches at East Somerville yards, in November 1947. One of B&M's 70 class P-2 Pacific locomotives will have an easy time with the train's four cars. This scene, now dominated by Interstate 93 and its exit ramps, was photographed from what today is the Austin Street/Charlestown Avenue bridge.

Plate 29 Long Island Rail Road, Morris Park terminal. *Long Island Rail Road*

In an image likely made during World War II, a cold winter day has the Long Island Rail Road's Morris Park engine terminal in Queens shrouded in steam as several engines are serviced for the busy commuter railroad. The 2-8-0 in the center accelerates away from the coaling tower, which is obscured by steam. At right, workers lubricate the driving rods of a G-class 4-6-0 parked over the inspection pit.

Plate 30 Canadian National 4-8-2 #6000, Pointe St. Charles Shops, Montreal. *Cecil Fray collection*

The 200-ton traveling crane at Canadian National's Pointe St. Charles Shops in Montreal is large enough to lift 177-ton 4-8-2 #6000 in a photo taken not long after the engine was built in 1923. The class U-1-a was the prototype for a group of 79 similar Mountain-type engines fielded by CN. Note the locomotive's unattached four-wheel, front-end "engine truck," still on the shop floor.

Plate 31 Denver & Rio Grande Western 2-8-2 #478, Durango, Colorado, January 1961. *Richard Steinheimer*

Wreathed in steam on a bitter cold January 1961 morning, Denver & Rio Grande Western 2-8-2 #478 leaves the roundhouse in Durango, Colorado, to shift empty stock cars in the yard for a later eastbound extra train. The narrow-gauge K-28 Mikado, built by Alco in 1923, had been relegated to yard duty in favor of larger K-36 and K-37 2-8-2s.

Plate 32 Chicago, Burlington & Quincy 2-10-2s, Edgemont, South Dakota, November 14, 1948. *G. B. Taylor*

The afternoon calm on November 14, 1948, is shattered by a pair of Chicago, Burlington & Quincy class M-2A 2-10-2s accelerating out of Edgemont, South Dakota, with a westbound "Banana Special," a solid train of 67 refrigerated boxcars loaded with bananas being shipped from the Gulf Coast to markets in the Pacific Northwest via CB&Q's connection with the Northern Pacific at Billings, Montana.

Plate 33 Louisville & Nashville engine terminal, Hazard, Kentucky, 1948. *Louisville & Nashville*

In 1948, construction crews at Louisville & Nashville's engine terminal in Hazard, Kentucky, work to enlarge the turntable to accommodate the latest 22 M-1 2-8-4s being built by Lima, designated for coal-hauling service on the Eastern Kentucky Division. The 98½-foot-long "Big Emmas" were the largest locomotives on the railroad.

Plate 34 Chicago & North Western 4-6-2s, Chicago, Illinois, August 24, 1953. *Wallace W. Abbey*

Sand pipes and coaling tower surround several engines from Chicago & North Western's huge fleet of E-class Pacifics congregating for service at the Chicago Avenue roundhouse during the midday lull between Windy City commuter assignments. By the time of the photo—August 24, 1953—the fast, high-drivered 4-6-2s had been pulled off long-distance trains and relegated strictly to suburban service.

Plate 35 Union Pacific 4-6-6-4 #3832, eastern Wyoming, 1956. *Robert Hale*

Union Pacific Challenger #3832 races across eastern Wyoming, headed from Cheyenne to North Platte, Nebraska, during its last months of operation in 1956. Union Pacific developed the 4-6-6-4 Challenger in 1936 and ultimately fielded 252 of the fast, powerful dual-service engines; Alco built the 3832 in 1937 as part of an order of 25 engines.

Plate 36 Union Pacific mixed train, near Smith's Ferry, Idaho, December 31, 1947. *R. H. Kindig*

Smoke and steam linger in the frigid air as Union Pacific train 386, a mixed train with five freight and two passenger cars, rolls at 30 mph through the Payette River Valley near Smith's Ferry, Idaho, on December 31, 1947. The oil-burning locomotive, 2-8-0 #284, will haul the train southward the entire 133 miles of UP's Idaho Northern Branch from Cascade to Nampa, near Boise.

Plate 37 Pennsylvania Railroad 4-8-2 #6761, Harrisburg, Pennsylvania, March 4, 1956. *Don Wood*

Time is running out on Pennsylvania Railroad steam as M1a Mountain #6761 departs Enola Yard and heads out on the Rockville Bridge over the Susquehanna River at Harrisburg, Pennsylvania, on March 4, 1956. The engineer keeps a sharp eye on the running gear as his 4-8-2 puts a wheel into the "Buffalo Box Car," a westbound freight with 114 loads for Williamsport and Renovo, where diesels will take over.

Plate 38 Nickel Plate Road 2-8-4 #814 with fireman filling tender, Cleveland, Ohio, 1958. *Art Hanford*

Nickel Plate Road fireman Myron Pease pulls the water-column spout over the tender of 2-8-4 #814 at the railroad's 75th Street yard on the east side of Cleveland. Alco built the engine for the Wheeling & Lake Erie, which became an NKP lessee in 1949. Soon after this spring 1958 photo the locomotive will be retired, along with all NKP steam.

Plate 39 Canadian National 4-8-4 #6234 in roundhouse, Hamilton, Ontario, December 1958. *Philip R. Hastings*

The 73-inch driving wheels and elegant running gear of a Canadian National 4-8-4 help frame a quartet of engine hostlers taking a coffee break from the evening's duties inside the CN roundhouse at Hamilton, Ontario, in December 1958. The still-hot locomotive, a U-2-g class Northern, will help keep the building warm for the night.

Plate 40 Chicago & North Western depot, Barrington, Illinois, March 1941. *Bill Rusk*

Morning mist enshrouds the small water tank at the end of Chicago & North Western's depot in Barrington, Illinois, on a weekday morning in March 1941. Before long, the empty brick platform will come alive with commuters awaiting the departure of another suburban train for North Western Station, 31.5 miles to the east in downtown Chicago.

Plate 41 Central Vermont 2-10-4 #703, Roxbury, Vermont, 1954–'55. *Paul A. Reynolds*

Central Vermont 2-10-4 #703 slogs up the long grade south of Roxbury, Vermont, on its way northbound from White River Junction to St. Albans with train 429 in the winter of 1954–'55. The CV had 10 of the Texas-type locomotives, the largest on the entire railroad and in all of New England, all built by Alco in 1928. The engineer has the side door behind him closed to take full advantage of the 703's distinctive all-weather cab.

Plate 42 Canadian Pacific 1200-class 4-6-2, Ottawa, Ontario, January 1955. *D. L. McQueen*

Canadian Pacific's *Dominion* passenger train departs Ottawa eastbound for Montreal on a bitter cold day in January 1955. A pair of F-unit diesels normally handles the train without difficulty, but on this day a 1200-class 4-6-2 is cut in behind the diesels to help cope with the 20-below weather. On an adjacent track, another 4-6-2 awaits a chance to depart with a local passenger train for Chalk River.

Plate 43 Canadian National 4-8-4 #6167, Toronto, Ontario, May 20, 1962. *Robert Gilmour*

The main rods, crankpin, and 73-inch driving wheels of Canadian National 4-8-4 #6167 reflect the afternoon light at CN's Spadina roundhouse in downtown Toronto following a May 20, 1962, steam excursion that originated in Fort Erie, Ontario. Montreal Locomotive Works built the U-2-e class Northern in 1940 and CN retired the engine in 1964. Today, the 6167 is displayed in Guelph, Ontario.

Plate 44 Union Pacific "Big Boy" engineer, east of Laramie, Wyoming, 1956. *Robert Hale*

The engineer of a Union Pacific 4-8-8-4 Big Boy is all concentration as he peers at the main line up ahead while running one of the giant articulated locomotives through Wyoming between Laramie and Cheyenne in 1956. The exterior windshield helps him lean out just far enough to see beyond the nearly 85-foot length of the locomotive's massive boiler.

Plate 45 Texas & Pacific station, Denton, Texas, September 21, 1941. *Charles M. Mizell Jr.*

The photographer, a self-described "scared kid with a cheap box camera," records the frenzy of a Texas & Pacific operator handing up handwritten "Form 19" train orders to the crew of a southbound Missouri-Kansas-Texas freight at Denton, Texas, on September 21, 1941. Standing back on the locomotive tender, the head brakeman exchanges waves with a local character known as Catfish. The T&P and MKT, or "Katy," shared this track north of Fort Worth.

Plate 46 Chicago & Eastern Illinois 4-6-2 at Dolton, Illinois. Trains *collection*

On a murky winter night in Chicago, a northbound Chicago & Eastern Illinois passenger train waits for a green signal at an interlocking tower at Yard Center, the railroad's main classification yard and engine terminal in the south-suburban town of Dolton. Steam exhaust from the 4-6-2's smokestack and electrical generator drift back over the train, which will soon end its run at Dearborn Station in Chicago's Loop.

Plate 47 Duluth & Northeastern 2-8-0 #16, Cloquet, Minnesota, August 7, 1961. *Philip R. Hastings*

The engineer of Duluth & Northeastern 2-8-0 #16 looks down at his fireman grabbing the ashpan lever to dump ashes at Cloquet, Minnesota, on August 7, 1961. The D&NE, a 12-mile remnant of a logging line linking Cloquet and Saginaw in Minnesota's north woods, attracted large numbers of photographers in the years leading up to its retirement of steam in 1964.

Plate 48 Pennsylvania Railroad 4-4-2 #759, Philadelphia, May 22, 1937. *E. Stanley Hart Jr.*

An air of urgency permeates the atmosphere on the upper Suburban level of Philadelphia's 30th Street Station on May 22, 1937, as Pennsylvania Railroad E6 Atlantic #759 prepares to lead a Pennsylvania-Reading Seashore Lines train out to Atlantic City, New Jersey. Steam escapes from the 4-4-2's turbogenerator and snifter valves as the engineer impatiently awaits the highball.

Plate 49 Baltimore & Ohio 4-6-2 #5300, Baltimore, Maryland, January 1952.
James P. Gallagher

Baltimore & Ohio #5300—the first Pacific in B&O's 1927 fleet of Baldwin-built P-7 class engines—awaits the highball from the conductor to pull train 21, the *Washingtonian*, out of Baltimore's Mount Royal Station in January 1952. Just ahead is the north portal of Baltimore Belt Line's Howard Street Tunnel, a 1.4-mile bore built in 1895 to avoid downtown congestion.

Plate 50 Santa Fe 4-4-2 #1440, south of Denver, Colorado, 1910.
L. C. McClure

Santa Fe 4-4-2 #1440 leads the Colorado & Southern's southbound *Pike's Peak Special* over a hand-cut stone culvert on the Joint Line between Denver and Colorado Springs in 1910. The C&S train is operating on trackage rights over Santa Fe, which shares the route with Denver & Rio Grande Western. Baldwin built the rakish Atlantic-type locomotive, a four-cylinder compound design, in 1907.

Plate 51 Erie Railroad, Starrucca Viaduct, Lanesboro, Pennsylvania. *Erie Railroad*

In an early-twentieth-century photograph, a Camelback locomotive hustles a westbound freight train over the Erie Railroad's magnificent Starrucca Viaduct at Lanesboro, Pennsylvania. The Erie built the double-track, 1,200-foot-long, 110-foot-high, 18-arch bridge in 1848 to span the quarter-mile-wide Starrucca Creek valley and complete its main line between Deposit and Binghamton, New York.

Plate 52 Illinois Central flooding at Memphis, Tennessee, April 1912. *Illinois Central*

A pair of Illinois Central locomotives, led by an 0-6-0 switcher, eases a passenger train through high water along the Mississippi River at Memphis during the historic flood of April 1912. Fast snowmelt in the upper Midwest contributed to the flooding throughout the Mississippi River basin, and in Memphis the water rose to 45 feet, far above the normal flood stage of 35 feet.

Plate 53 Illinois Central flooding at Helm, Mississippi, May 9, 1927. *Illinois Central*

An Illinois Central supervisor crouches precariously on washed-out track to mark one of countless places where the railroad was destroyed in the Great Mississippi Flood of 1927, the worst inundation in the history of the United States. The photo was made May 9, 1927, near Helm, Mississippi, just north of Leland. The flood forced more than 630,000 people to flee their homes and ultimately covered 27,000 square miles in 10 states.

Plate 54 Illinois Central engine terminal, Centralia, Illinois, August 1, 1912. *Illinois Central*

In the quintessential Illinois Central town of Centralia, Illinois — named for the railroad when incorporated in 1853 — workers shovel ballast from a gondola on August 1, 1912, as part of the construction of a new yard and locomotive facility. Under construction in the middle distance is a new water tank; farther beyond, a coaling tower is ready for service.

Plate 55 Baltimore & Ohio, Bollman truss bridge, Harpers Ferry, West Virginia. *B&O Railroad*

An ornate symbol of the Baltimore & Ohio Railroad— a skewed Bollman truss bridge—crosses the power canal serving a small hydroelectric plant at Harpers Ferry, West Virginia. Designed by B&O engineer Wendel Bollman, this iron span was constructed in the 1870s. It was commonly called a suspension truss because the deck was suspended from tension members connected to the top chord. B&O had more than 100 Bollman-style bridges, most of them east of Harpers Ferry.

Plate 56 Oneida & Western 2-8-0 #28, northeastern Tennessee, 1954. *Philip R. Hastings*

At dusk on an evening in the summer of 1954 an Oneida & Western train crew head back to their engine for the saddest assignment of all: scrapping the 38-mile short line in rural northeast Tennessee, ripping up the rails behind their 2-8-0, 39-foot section by 39-foot section. Soon, the track between Oneida and Jamestown will be gone forever.

Plate 57 Canadian National 4-6-0 #1576, at Palmerston, Ontario, February 1958.
Jim Shaughnessy

Canadian National 4-6-0 #1576 has backed the consist of its mixed train onto a yard track and is ready to head for the roundhouse at Palmerston, Ontario, on an overcast afternoon in February 1958. Located about 90 miles west of Toronto, Palmerston was the hub of a network of CN branch lines still using small steam locomotives into the late 1950s. Today, there are no railroads left in town.

Plate 58 Duluth & Northeastern 2-8-0 #27, Cloquet, Minnesota, January 1962.
John Gruber

The brakeman on a Duluth & Northeastern switch job endures the brutal cold of a January 1962 day as 2-8-0 #27 backs his train toward the caboose while working at the Wood Conversion Co. plant in Cloquet, Minnesota. Built to serve the logging industry, the 12.6-mile D&NE stuck with steam locomotives in regular service until 1964.

Plate 59 Santa Fe 4-8-4 #3781, Canyon Diablo, Arizona, 1947. *Santa Fe Railway*

Santa Fe train 3, the westbound *California Limited*, eases across the old bridge at Canyon Diablo, Arizona, during construction of a new 544-foot span featuring a 300-foot hinged arch. The photo was taken not long before the new bridge opened in 1947. At the head end of the train is 4-8-4 #3781, built in 1941 by Baldwin, its characteristic stack extension raised to lift smoke high enough to clear the cab.

Plate 60 Central Railroad of New Jersey, Terminal semaphore signals, Jersey City, New Jersey, 1967. *David Plowden*

Tracks, slip switches, and semaphores leading into the Central Railroad of New Jersey's terminal at Jersey City are a study in geometry in a view looking west from an adjacent signal bridge in the early 1960s. The terminal was often called Communipaw, so named for a cove off New York Harbor.

Plate 61 Illinois Central 0-8-0 #3541, Champaign, Illinois, November 30, 1958. *Ed Wojtas*

The roundhouse at Champaign, Illinois, is in its last week of steam as Illinois Central 0-8-0 #3541 pauses by the water column late at night on November 30, 1958. The locomotive, one of only three steam switchers still hanging on at the engine terminal, has just pushed a Santa Claus passenger special into the passenger depot. Within a week the trio will be sent to IC's shops in Paducah, Kentucky, to be scrapped.

Plate 62 Norfolk & Western 4-8-2 #104, Bristol, Virginia, 1957. *O. Winston Link*

Nighttime in the engine terminal at Bristol, Virginia, in 1957: The engineer of Norfolk & Western K1-class 4-8-2 #104 carefully positions his locomotive so his fireman, standing on the tender, can place the water spout over the tender tank. On the adjacent track, a much smaller M-class 4-8-0 off N&W's celebrated Abingdon Branch lifts the pops on its safety valves.

Plate 63 New York Central 4-6-4 #5249, Harmon, New York, 1949. *Ed Nowak*

One of New York Central's celebrated Hudson passenger engines eases off the turntable at Harmon, New York, where for decades NYC exchanged steam for electric locomotives used in Manhattan. The #5249 in this 1949 image is a J-1a-e, one of 145 delivered by Alco between 1927 and 1931. The Central pioneered the development of the Hudson-type 4-6-4 and, with 275 such locomotives, had by far North America's largest fleet.

Plate 64 Terminal interlocking tower, 1944. *Union Switch & Signal*

In a 1944 publicity photo, an operator in the interlocking tower of an unidentified major terminal poses with the tools of his trade: a skein of "armstrong" levers used to control switches and signals; a model board above, diagramming the interlocking; wooden train-order hoops hung by the door; a scissors-mounted company telephone; and, at his right hand, a brass telegraph key.

Plate 65 Canadian National 4-6-4, Oakville, Ontario, February 15, 1958. *Jim Shaughnessy*

A Canadian National 4-6-4 speeds across CN's bridge over Sixteen Mile Creek in the western Toronto suburb of Oakville, hauling a westbound passenger train across the railroad's Oakville Subdivision on a snowy February 15, 1958. The locomotive is one of CN's five 5700-series Hudsons in the K-5-a class, built in September and October 1930 by Montreal Locomotive Works.

Plate 66 Southern Pacific track worker, San Francisco, California, 1950. *Richard Steinheimer*

A Southern Pacific track worker is undeterred by the fog of a 1950 morning as he walks SP's Coast Line near one of several tunnels in South San Francisco. He is carrying two classic tools of his trade, a track wrench and an inspection lantern, as he approaches suspended telltale ropes, warning anyone riding on a freight car of the approach of a tunnel portal no more than 100 feet away.

Plate 67 Central Railroad of New Jersey bridge, Lehighton, Pennsylvania, 1965. *David Plowden*

A study in steel: a pair of track workers is framed by Jersey Central's truss bridge carrying its main line to Scranton, Pennsylvania, over four tracks leading into Lehigh Valley Railroad's Packerton Yard at Lehighton, in eastern Pennsylvania, in 1965. The CNJ bridge was constructed in 1906 on masonry abutments that dated to 1870 and was reinforced in 1921.

Plate 68 Rock Island 4-8-2, Clinton, Oklahoma, late 1940s. *Joe Conn*

Lit by flashbulbs and a full moon, a Rock Island passenger train pauses at Clinton, Oklahoma, in the late 1940s. Dimly visible in the soft light, their lanterns tracing bright streaks in the moonlight, crewmen inspect the locomotive, an M-50-class 4-8-2. This was Rock Island's "Choctaw Route" main line linking Memphis, Little Rock, and Oklahoma City with Amarillo, Texas, and Tucumcari, New Mexico. On the overhead bridge is Santa Fe's former Kansas City, Mexico & Orient line between Chillicothe, Texas, and Cherokee, Oklahoma.

Plate 69 Southern Railway 4-8-2, Dendron, North Carolina, 1944. *Frank Clodfelter*

A Southern Railway 4-8-2 on a westbound passenger train in 1944 digs in above Dendron, North Carolina, where the railroad doubles over itself to gain elevation between Old Fort and Ridgecrest, deep in the Blue Ridge Mountains. This tortuous piece of the Southern has grades as steep as 2.2 percent and uses 12 miles of railroad to cover 3 miles as the crow flies. The photographer was a locomotive engineer on this line.

Plate 70 Graham County Railroad Shay #1926, Nantahala Gorge, North Carolina, September 1962. *J. E. Bradley*

North Carolina's Nantahala Gorge, deep in the Great Smoky Mountains, echoes with the chattering exhaust of Graham County Railroad's Shay locomotive #1926 as it works upgrade from its Southern Railway connection at Topton with three freight cars for Robbinsville on a Saturday morning in September 1962. The 12-mile short line ceased operations in 1970.

Plate 71 Central Railroad of New Jersey, Jersey City Terminal, May 18, 1953. *Philip R. Hastings*

A commuter strolls onto the quiet Track 13 platform at Jersey City Terminal to catch his train, Central Railroad of New Jersey's 12:38 p.m. departure for Dunellen, approximately 26 miles to the west. Although the passenger probably isn't aware of it, on this day, May 18, 1953, a Camelback 4-6-0 is substituting for his train's usual diesel.

Plate 72 Pennsylvania Railroad station, Harrisburg, Pennsylvania, April 1948. *Linn H. Westcott*

Passengers and a platform repair crew gather under the Pennsylvania Railroad's Harrisburg station concourse in an April 1948 view looking west. At right, a B1 electric switcher attends to an inbound commuter train. PRR electrification reached Pennsylvania's capital city in 1938, after which all trains exchanged electric locomotives for steam and, later, diesel.

Plate 73–84 Vignettes from the Lehigh Valley Railroad and the New Haven Railroad, 1941–'42. *Noel Hiram Deeks*

The photographer, an assistant to noted photographer and curator Edward Steichen, recorded these scenes of Lehigh Valley steam locomotives at the LV shops in Sayre, Pennsylvania, and vignettes of the New Haven Railroad at Danbury and Branchville, Connecticut. NH agent John English was photographed in the depot at Branchville amid the tools of his trade: a scissors phone and levers to operate the train-order signals.

Plate 85 Virginia & Truckee 4-6-0 #27, Steamboat Springs, Nevada, 1948. *Lucius Beebe*

In 1948, in the waning days of Nevada's famed Virginia & Truckee Railroad, Ten-Wheeler #27 rumbles along near Steamboat Springs with the morning mixed train from Reno to Carson City, the state capital. The locomotive was built in 1913 by Baldwin and taken out of service shortly after the photo was made. Two years later, on May 31, 1950, the railroad was abandoned. The 4-6-0 is preserved at the Nevada State Railroad Museum in Carson City.

Plate 86 Baltimore & Ohio 2-8-2 #4493, near Dayton, Ohio, January 1956. *J. Parker Lamb*

Baltimore & Ohio 2-8-2 #4493 slogs through wet snow on its way eastward from Dayton and Xenia, Ohio, to Washington Court House with a local freight in January 1956. Equipped with a trademark B&O Vanderbilt tender, the class Q-4B Mikado was built by Baldwin in 1922 and, at the time of the photo, had little more than a year left before its retirement. Successor CSX abandoned this part of B&O's old Toledo Division in 1982.

Plate 87 Northern Pacific 4-8-4, Bozeman, Montana, February 13, 1941. *E. R. Augustin Jr.*

A Northern Pacific 4-8-4 marches up the NP main line adjacent to U.S. 10 on the eastbound ascent to Bozeman Pass, elevation 5,702 feet, in the Rocky Mountains between Bozeman and Livingston, Montana. The train, which has a helper locomotive on the rear end, includes a number of refrigerated "reefer" boxcars on this February 13, 1941.

Plate 88 Southern Pacific shops, Sacramento, California, 1941. *Southern Pacific*

Shop workers tend to a steam locomotive in for an overhaul at Southern Pacific's main shops in Sacramento, California, in 1941. Above, a boilermaker crouches inside the smokebox and uses an electric arc welder to repair the steam delivery pipes linking the front-end throttle with the cylinders and valves. Below him, a machinist works on the fireman's-side main cylinder.

Plate 89 Canadian National 0-8-0 #8421, Toronto, Ontario, July 4, 1958. *Bruce R. Meyer*

The front end of Canadian National #8421, an 0-8-0 switcher, shows a patina of grime and grease as it awaits assignment under steam in the huge Spadina roundhouse near downtown Toronto on July 4, 1958. The class P-5-j engine was constructed in 1923 by Brooks Locomotive Works, a component of Alco. The roundhouse primarily serviced locomotives working in and out of nearby Toronto Union Station.

Plate 90 Southern Pacific 4-8-8-2 at Saugus, California, 1952. *M. M. Deaderick*

A late afternoon rain has washed the platform of the Southern Pacific station at Saugus, California, north of Los Angeles in the San Fernando Valley, as an AC cab-forward 4-8-8-2 locomotive heads out of town with a westbound freight in 1952. This is SP's main line north from Los Angeles to Palmdale and Mojave, then beyond to the San Joaquin Valley.

Plate 91 Canadian National 4-8-4, London, Ontario, late 1930s. *Canadian National*

An engine wiper at Canadian National's Rectory Street roundhouse in London, Ontario, cleans the running gear and 77-inch driving wheels of one of CN's five 6400-series streamlined class U-4-b 4-8-4s in a late 1930s image. The spray-washing technique utilizes a mixture of steam-heated water combined with a small amount of oil to cut through the dirt and grease on the rods and wheels.

Plate 92 Pennsylvania Railroad 4-6-2 #830, South Amboy, New Jersey, January 1, 1957. *Don Wood*

Pennsylvania K4s #830 opens up its cylinder cocks at South Amboy, New Jersey, as it prepares for a commuter run on PRR's New York & Long Branch Division, owned by PRR and Jersey Central. It's only 10 degrees above zero on this January 1, 1957, and the locomotive is in its last months of service. It is one of 425 K4s engines built either by Baldwin or PRR between 1914 and 1928.

Plate 93 Canadian National 4-6-2 #5288 near Sherbrooke, Quebec, February 1957. *Jim Shaughnessy*

A Canadian National 4-6-2 hurries northbound out of Sherbrooke, Quebec, toward Richmond along the Saint-François River, with the morning passenger train for Montreal in February 1957. The 5288 was built by Montreal Locomotive Works as part of an order in 1918 and 1919 for 45 class J-7-a Pacifics for CN predecessor Canadian Government Railways.

Plate 94 Norfolk & Western 4-8-2, Hagerstown, Maryland, March 1956. *O. Winston Link*

On a snowy March night in 1956, a Norfolk & Western 4-8-2 clatters over the intersecting Western Maryland tracks at Hager interlocking in Hagerstown, Maryland. The engine is backing up from the roundhouse to the Hagerstown station to pick up cars delivered by the Pennsylvania Railroad, to be added to a southbound train headed down N&W's Shenandoah Division to Roanoke.

Plate 95 Pennsylvania-Reading Seashore Lines 4-4-2 #6085, Camden, New Jersey, 1949. *John Fulginiti*

Safety valves are lifting on E6 Atlantic #6085 at Pennsylvania-Reading Seashore Lines' coaling tower at Camden, New Jersey, in 1949. The locomotive is one of 9 ultra-fast 4-4-2s transferred from the Pennsylvania Railroad to affiliate PRSL for commuter service out of Camden and express trains from Philadelphia to Atlantic City. PRSL was jointly owned by PRR and the Reading Company.

Plate 96 Chicago & North Western E-class 4-6-2, Milwaukee, Wisconsin, 1940. *Linn H. Westcott*

An engine hostler at Chicago & North Western's Erie Street roundhouse and coach yard in Milwaukee keeps an eye on the level in the tank as an E-class 4-6-2 takes on water in 1940. The engine terminal, located beside Lake Michigan near the entrance to Milwaukee's harbor, mainly serviced locomotives working in and out of C&NW's elaborate passenger station on the city's lakefront.

Plate 97 Washing Nickel Plate Road 2-8-2 being washed, Frankfort, Indiana, 1943. *William M. Rittase*

Female railroaders at the Nickel Plate Road's engine terminal in Frankfort, Indiana, use long-handled brushes and soap to wash down the tender of a 2-8-2 parked at the roundhouse in 1943. Like most railroads during World War II, the NKP hired hundreds of women to replace the approximately 3,000 men the railroad lost to the armed services from 1942 through 1945.

Plate 98 New York Central engine terminal, Harmon, New York, 1920s. *Fred Eidenbenz*

A 4-6-2 is still the queen of New York Central passenger power in this photo taken at Harmon, New York, just ahead of the 1927 arrival of the famed Hudson 4-6-4s that would replace the Pacifics. Parked in rows behind the live 4-6-2 are several stored 0-6-0s, their smokestacks dutifully covered. Other features of a large-scale engine terminal include the trio of water towers and the long cinder pit, here being cleaned out by a steam shovel.

Plate 99 New York Central engine terminal, Rensselaer, New York, 1930s. *New York Central*

New York Central's locomotive facility in Rensselaer, New York, across the Hudson River from Albany, is alive with activity in a 1930s-era photo. At center, a concrete-and-steel coaling wharf (built by the Gifford-Wood Co. in 1923) stretches over four tracks, fed by coal hopper cars unloading at left. At right, switchers congregate around a pair of water tanks. Coaling of engines has been momentarily suspended as a track crew installs new ties in the foreground.

Plate 100 Denver, Northwestern & Pacific train, above Plainview, Colorado, early 1900s.
H. H. Buckwalter collection, Ph.00057 (Scan #20030040), History Colorado, Denver, Colorado

Nearing South Boulder Canyon on Colorado's Front Range, train 101 of the Denver, Northwestern & Pacific climbs between Tunnels 6 and 7 above Plainview in a glass-plate-negative image from the early 1900s. Financier David Moffat built the line over 11,000-foot Rollins Pass beginning in 1902 as a direct route west from Denver. The DNW&P was later reorganized as the Denver & Salt Lake, ultimately to became part of Denver & Rio Grande.

Plate 101 Central Vermont 2-8-0, at Rouses Point, New York, 1955. *Jim Shaughnessy*

Central Vermont's daily local freight train creeps across the trestle over the northern tip of Lake Champlain at Rouses Point, New York, near the northwestern corner of Vermont, where CV connects with the Delaware & Hudson and the Rutland Railroad. A 2-8-0 has charge of the 6-car train on a quiet day in the summer of 1955.

Plate 102 Canadian National station, Niagara Falls, Ontario, August 24, 1953.
Wallace W. Abbey

Two business travelers cross paths on the platform of the Canadian National–Wabash station at Niagara Falls, Ontario, after the arrival at 10:58 a.m. of train 101 from Toronto and Hamilton on August 24, 1953. The train includes a through sleeper and buffet/parlor car from Montreal. CN ran 8 to 10 trains per day along the 82-mile corridor between Toronto and Niagara Falls.

Plate 103 Chicago, Burlington & Quincy station stop, McCook, Nebraska, 1948.
Philip Morris, for Bendix Radio

A lone traveler witnesses the 4 a.m. stop of a Chicago, Burlington & Quincy passenger train—most likely the eastbound *Ak-Sar-Ben Zephyr*—at McCook, Nebraska, in 1948. McCook is at milepost 283 from Omaha, so the train is only a quarter of the way into its 1,034-mile journey from Denver to Chicago Union Station.

Plate 104 Denver & Rio Grande Western yard, Durango, Colorado, January 30, 1961.
Richard Steinheimer

Armed with pry bar, a brakeman walks the rooftops of narrow-gauge boxcars at the east end of Denver & Rio Grande Western's yard in Durango, Colorado, on the frosty morning of January 30, 1961. Soon, despite the protestations of balky pipes and frozen brake rigging, 2-8-2 #478 will head out with an eastbound freight train.

Plate 105 East Broad Top roundhouse, Orbisonia, Pennsylvania, July 10, 1952. *Philip R. Hastings*

On a quiet night in July 1952, three live narrow-gauge engines, 2-8-2s #14, #15, and #16, are tucked inside the East Broad Top Railroad & Coal Company roundhouse at Orbisonia, in the mountains of south-central Pennsylvania. At its height, EBT's empire covered 60 miles of track and 33 miles of main line, but the coal business ended in 1956. The north end of the railroad was revived in 1961 as a tourist line, and the Orbisonia shops complex has been preserved.

Plate 106 Norfolk & Western Y6-class 2-8-8-2s, Iaeger, West Virginia, March 26, 1959.
Bruce R. Meyer

The engine crews have their assignments from the yard office and a pair of massive Norfolk & Western Y6 2-8-8-2s are ready for the day's work out of Iaeger, West Virginia, deep in the Tug Fork Valley on the railroad's Pocahontas Division. It's dawn on March 26, 1959, and the celebrated homebuilt N&W locomotives have only a few more months until retirement.

Plate 107 Canadian Pacific 2-8-0 #3554, Chipman, New Brunswick, October 1953.
Philip R. Hastings

A morning mist from the Salmon River has settled over Chipman, New Brunswick, as Canadian Pacific 2-8-0 #3554 ventures out of the enginehouse for the day's work switching coal mines at Minto some 12 miles to the southwest. The CP branches around Chipman remained a bastion of steam when the scene was recorded in October 1953.

Plate 108 Canadian Pacific 2-8-2 #5214, Bayview Junction, Ontario, January 28, 1959. *Frank Barry*

Canadian Pacific 2-8-2 #5214 blasts upgrade under the York Boulevard bridge at Bayview Junction, Ontario, with an eastbound freight train from Hamilton on January 28, 1959. Overlooking Hamilton Harbor on Lake Ontario, the complex and busy wye-shaped junction is where CP trains join the Canadian National main line into Toronto.

Plate 109 Southern Railway 4-6-2 #1407, Lynchburg, Virginia, May 1950. *H. Reid*

Southern Railway 4-6-2 #1407, one of the railroad's premier green-and-gold Ps4-class Pacifics, enters an underpass in Lynchburg, Virginia, with a mainline passenger train in May 1950. The engine was built by Baldwin in 1928, one of 64 such USRA-design heavy Pacifics fielded by Southern and its subsidiaries the Cincinnati, New Orleans & Texas Pacific and the Alabama Great Southern.

Plate 110 Baltimore & Ohio EM-1 2-8-8-4 #7605 at Painesville, Ohio, 1955. *Jim Shaughnessy*

Displaying white "extra" flags for its next run, Baltimore & Ohio class EM-1 2-8-8-4 #7605 pauses in 1955 outside the enginehouse in Painesville, Ohio. B&O's coal-hauling Lake Branch in northeast Ohio linked Warren with Fairport Harbor on Lake Erie and was a hotbed for these articulated engines in their last years of service. The railroad bought 30 of the gigantic EM-1s from Baldwin in 1944–'45.

Plate 111 Chesapeake & Ohio 2-6-6-6 #1624, Thurmond, West Virginia, 1955. *Philip R. Hastings*

The tiny commercial district of Thurmond, West Virginia, is rattled by the exhaust of Chesapeake & Ohio 2-6-6-6 #1624 wrestling 91 loads of eastbound coal through town in 1955. The 1624 was one of 60 mammoth Allegheny-type engines built for C&O by Lima Locomotive Works between 1941 and 1948. Today, Thurmond is in the heart of the New River Gorge National River recreational area.

Plate 112 Rock Island passenger train at Sheffield, Illinois, August 2, 1911. *Roy Campbell collection*

The town of Sheffield, Illinois, comes to life for the mid-day arrival of an eastbound Rock Island passenger train from Rock Island, Illinois, on August 2, 1911. Essential details of the American small-town scene include the local grain elevator, train-order semaphore, water column, mail and express on the platform, and a gaggle of towns-people turning to watch the arriving train.

Plate 113 Louisville & Nashville 4-6-2, Venedy, Illinois, 1953. *Warren Stricker*

Louisville & Nashville's train 51 accelerates away from the diminutive station near Venedy, Illinois, behind a 4-6-2 after dropping off and picking up mail and express on a foggy early-spring morning in 1953. The all-day, all-stops local train left St. Louis early in the morning, headed east via L&N's line through Evansville, Indiana, and is sched-uled to arrive in Nashville, Tennessee, in the evening. The L&N depended heavily on 4-6-2s, with 146 Pacific types in 11 classes on the roster.

Plate 114 Boston & Maine 4-6-2 #3623, White River Junction, Vermont, late 1940s. *Philip R. Hastings*

Framed by an ancient "multi-ball" signal, Boston & Maine 4-6-2 #3623 leads the Montreal-Boston *Ambassador* over the intersection with the Central Vermont at White River Junction, Vermont, in a late-1940s image. In the background, a southbound CV freight train waits for the passenger train to clear.

Plate 115 Canadian National *Continental Limited* at Saskatoon, Saskatchewan, 1952. *W. A. Akin Jr.*

Dusk has settled at 9 p.m. on a summer evening in 1952 as Canadian National's westbound *Continental Limited* pauses for 30 minutes at Saskatoon, Saskatchewan. Up at the head end of the transcontinental train, the locomo-tive has stopped just short of the concrete coaling tower, where it will pause for water and fuel before departing for points west.

Plate 116 Baltimore & Ohio switchers, Brunswick, Maryland, September 1953. *James P. Gallagher*

On a frosty morning in September 1953, a pair of Balti-more & Ohio steam switchers is ready for the day's work at the east end of the railroad's sprawling yards in Bruns-wick, Maryland, along the Potomac River 74 miles west of Baltimore. The B&O built the yard in 1891 near the strategic junction of its two main lines from Baltimore and Washington, D.C., to the west.

Plate 117 Central Vermont 2-8-0 #501, Brattleboro, Vermont, 1956. *Jim Shaughnessy*

Central Vermont 2-8-0 #501, freshly loaded with coal, simmers on the 70-foot turntable at the roundhouse in Brattleboro, Vermont, on a spring evening in 1956. Visible through the windows is another CV locomotive awaiting servicing. Located in the southern part of the state, Brattleboro was a key engine terminal on CV, a longtime subsidiary of Canadian National.

Plate 118 Southern Pacific engineer, Mojave, California, 1948. *Ward Kimball*

In one of railroading's oldest rituals, Southern Pacific locomotive engineer Boscom Farrow leans out from the cab window of his northbound 4-8-2 as the station operator at Mojave, California, "hoops up" paper train orders, advising the engine crew of slow orders ahead for track work. The 1948 image is one of several taken on the last day of Farrow's 48-year career on Southern Pacific. Photographer Ward Kimball was an Academy Award–winning animator for Walt Disney.

Plate 119 Norfolk & Western terminal, Norfolk, Virginia, January 1957. *Mallory Hope Ferrell*

Surrounded by shovels, wrenches, rags, and other tools of the trade, engine hostlers take a break next to a hot coal stove on a cold January 1957 afternoon at Norfolk & Western's sprawling export terminal in Norfolk, Virginia. The workers have found shelter from the wind by standing between a pair of hulking A-class 2-6-6-4s.

Plate 120 New York Central 4-8-2 #3005, Galion, Ohio, September 1955. *Philip R. Hastings*

New York Central engineer John Hitchko is impatient as he looks back from Mohawk #3005 and awaits the high-ball after taking coal and water for his eastbound freight train at Galion, Ohio, in September 1955. Water drips from the 4-8-2's injector as Hitchko chats with one of his crew. Based out of Cleveland, Hitchko had a 47-year career with NYC.

Plate 121 New York Central 4-6-4- #5403, Mattoon, Illinois, September 1954. *Philip R. Hastings*

The fireman on New York Central 4-6-4 #5403 is all business as his engine accelerates toward 80 mph west-bound from Mattoon, Illinois, with a mail and express train for St. Louis in September 1954. Soon the pho-tographer and his driver, *Trains* editor David P. Morgan, pacing on Illinois Highway 16, will be left behind. Steam is on the wane: on this day, 5403 is the only active steam locomotive on NYC west of Indianapolis.

Plate 122 Canadian National caboose interior, New Brunswick, 1955. *Philip R. Hastings*

Safe from the frigid winter weather, the conductor of a Canadian National freight train tends to the time-honored chore of examining his wheel reports as his brakeman takes a break for tea inside their caboose in New Bruns-wick in 1955. The caboose was the conductor's office on the road and a place where the crew could make coffee, cook a meal, or otherwise escape the elements.

Plate 123 Union Pacific 4-8-8-4 #4009 near Dale Junction, Wyoming, August 20, 1957. *Jim Shaughnessy*

One of Union Pacific's giant 4-8-8-4 "Big Boy" locomo-tives hauls a long freight train up the east side of the Continental Divide near Dale Junction on Sherman Hill, between Laramie and Cheyenne, Wyoming. The train is using the new lower-elevation line built after World War II, mostly for westbound traffic. Alco built 25 of the Big Boys for UP, 20 in 1941 and another 5 in 1944.

Plate 124 Maine Central mixed train at Crawford Notch, New Hampshire, 1952. *Frank Clodfelter*

A trainman looks back from the rear platform of the lone coach on a Maine Central mixed train as it passes the Mount Willard Section House near Crawford Notch in the White Mountains of New Hampshire in 1952. Built in 1887 as a depot, the building served most of its life as the residence for the local section foreman. Today this stretch of railroad survives as part of the Conway Scenic tourist line.

Plate 125 Southern Railway 2-8-2 #4505, Saluda Grade, North Carolina, August 3, 1950. *August A. Thieme Jr.*

Slogging through an August 3, 1950, downpour, Southern Railway 2-8-2 #4505 blasts it way up North Carolina's fabled Saluda Grade over the Blue Ridge toward Asheville with a westbound freight train. Credited as the steepest segment of main line in North America, Saluda at its toughest climbs 4.24 percent for 2.6 miles.

Plate 126 Canadian National 4-8-4 #6147, London, Ontario, late 1930s. *Canadian National Railway*

Canadian National 4-8-4 #6147, one of 20 U-2-c class engines delivered by Montreal Locomotive Works to CN in 1929, rolls through the wash rack at the Rectory Street roundhouse in London, Ontario, in a late-1930s photo-graph. The wash rack typically used a combination of high-pressure steam and solvent to cut dirt and grease.

Plate 127 Illinois Central 2-8-2, Cairo, Illinois, 1950. *Henry J. McCord*

An Illinois Central 2-8-2 leads a northbound freight train over the Ohio River into Cairo, Illinois, on the original truss-and-deck span built by the railroad in 1889 and designed by prominent bridge engineer George S. Morison. This photo was taken just before construction began on the new IC bridge, opened in 1952. Visible in the fore-ground is track of the New York Central's "Egyptian" line to Cairo.

Plate 128 Wabash Railroad 4-4-0 #659, Chicago, Illinois, June 12, 1931. *A. W. Johnson*

The skyline of Chicago's South Loop serves as the backdrop for Wabash 4-4-0 #659 and train 39, departing Dearborn Station for Orland Park as a commuter train and beyond to Decatur as an all-stops local, on June 12, 1931. Built in 1899 by Burnham, Williams & Co., the ancient Eight-Wheeler was already a rare engine at the time the photograph was made.

Plate 129 Chicago & North Western 4-6-2 #2901, Madison, Wisconsin, July 9, 1955. *William D. Middleton*

Chicago & North Western train 504, a Chicago-bound express behind class E-2 Pacific #2901, approaches Monona Tower in Madison, Wisconsin, on July 9, 1955. The unusual interlocking tower was in the middle of Lake Monona on the city's south side and controlled the cross-ing of the C&NW and Milwaukee Road, both on cause-ways. The tower was in the process of being dismantled when the photograph was made.

Plate 130 Southern Pacific cabooses, Roseville Yard, California, 1958. *Philip R. Hastings*

Nearly every type of Southern Pacific caboose—wooden cupola, all-steel cupola, all-steel bay window—is parked on the caboose track and visible through the terminal superintendent's office window at Roseville Yard, outside Sacramento, California, in a spring 1958 image. Roseville was the SP's main freight classification facility on the Sacramento Division.

Plate 131 Rock Island station at Decorah, Iowa, 1950s. *Philip R. Hastings*

Interior lights lend warmth to the Rock Island depot in Decorah, Iowa, on a winter night in the 1950s. This obscure branch line reached 140 miles from Cedar Rapids into the northeast corner of the state at Decorah, which also had service from a Milwaukee Road branch. Rock Island ended passenger service to Decorah in 1963 and abandoned the branch altogether a few months later. The depot survives today as an apartment house.

Plate 132 Southern Pacific 4-8-8-2 #4165, Colton, California, 1951. *Richard Steinheimer*

The water column at Southern Pacific's terminal in Colton, California, frames one of the railroad's magnificent AC-class cab-forward 4-8-8-2 articulated locomotives, called upon this night in 1951 to assist train 44, the *Cherokee*, up Beaumont Hill to the east. SP was a pioneer in the development of the cab-forward design, which put the crew at the front of the engine so they could avoid breathing dangerous fumes in SP's numerous long tunnels.

Plate 133 Denver & Rio Grande Western 2-8-2 #483, Cumbres Pass, Colorado, early 1960s. *Richard Steinheimer*

In an early 1960s photograph, the full moon of a fall evening looks down on Denver & Rio Grande Western narrow-gauge 2-8-2 #483 blasting upgrade with a west-bound extra a few miles west of the 10,015-foot summit in Cumbres Pass in southern Colorado. After cresting the pass, the train will ease downgrade into the railroad's terminal in Chama, New Mexico.

Plate 134 Baltimore & Ohio yards, Buckhannon, West Virginia, 1949. *H. Reid*

A hostler at the Baltimore & Ohio yards in Buckhannon, West Virginia, is framed by steam from the cylinder cocks of a 2-8-2 in a 1949 photo. Buckhannon was home to a roundhouse and locomotive shops of B&O's Monongah Division, which penetrated south from the division point of Grafton into coalfields of the Allegheny foothills in the north-central part of the state.

Plate 135 Canadian Pacific 4-6-4 #2838, London, Ontario, August 1959. *Ted Rose*

Once reserved for prestigious passenger trains and facing imminent retirement, Canadian Pacific Royal Hudson #2838 pauses at the coaling dock at London, Ontario, on an August 1959 evening after coming off an eastbound freight train. CP fielded 45 of the streamlined 4-6-4s, designated "Royal" by the presence of a crown insignia on the running-board skirt above the cylinders.

Plate 136 Maine Central 4-6-0 #371, Crawford Notch, New Hampshire, October 1952. *Philip R. Hastings*

Maine Central Ten-Wheeler #371 labors up the stiff grade through Crawford Notch in New Hampshire's rugged White Mountains, lugging an eastbound freight train in October 1952. The Notch, now a historic site, was a steep, narrow gorge of the Saco River that accommodated MEC's Portland Division main line, the railroad's principal route for traffic to and from the west.

Plate 137 Georgia-Pacific Shay #19, Log Cabin, West Virginia. *W. G. Gordon*

Spring rains have flooded Lilly Fork at Log Cabin, deep in the mountains of central West Virginia, as Shay locomotive #19 eases across the swollen creek with loaded log racks headed for Georgia-Pacific's sawmill complex at Swandale. The 65-ton geared Shay engine was built by Lima in 1905 and survives today on display in Harrod, Ohio.

Plate 138 Canadian Pacific 4-6-2 #2457, Sherbrooke, Quebec, November 1953. *Philip R. Hastings*

The depot platform at Sherbrooke, Quebec, is busy on a foggy morning in November 1953 as Quebec Central 4-6-2 #2556 sits on the far track with train 1 for Quebec City, awaiting the arrival of Canadian Pacific train 39 from Saint John, New Brunswick, just pulling into the station behind 4-6-2 #2457.

Plate 139 Wichita Falls & Southern 2-8-0 #30, Ranger, Texas, 1945. *Lucius Beebe*

The fireman on Wichita Falls & Southern 2-8-0 #30 keeps the water column in position over the tender at the desolate water tank in Ranger, Texas, in a 1945 photo. Always a hand-to-mouth operation, the WF&S wandered for 170 miles through the rolling country of north Texas between Wichita Falls and Dublin, mostly transporting crude oil and drilling equipment. The railroad was abandoned in 1954.

Editors' Note & Acknowledgments

Jeff Brouws
Wendy Burton

Norfolk & Western 2-8-8-2 #2133 on rear of coal drag cresting the Blue Ridge mountains west of Roanoke, Virginia, October 1957. *William E. Warden*

AS THE BOOK'S EDITORS and part-time researchers we were given the wonderful opportunity to delve into the Kalmbach Publishing Co.'s David P. Morgan Memorial Library archive for two weeks during the winter of 2013 and spring of 2014. Because it is a working archive and not a repository of fragile fine art photographs, we were able to handle the prints quickly and confidently to make our initial edit, not the normal situation when the archival materials are of the "handle-with-white-gloves-only" variety.

To make the book and our explorations through the library manageable we decided this volume would contain only images of steam. Because railroading's steam era lasted approximately 135 years, it was essential to include early and late examples from the visual record. John Gruber's marvelous 35mm image, taken in 1962 of Duluth & Northeastern's 2-8-0 shuffling freight cars in Cloquet, Minnesota (page 95), is the late-period entry for our timeline, while A. J. Russell's 10 x 13 glass-plate construction picture, made on the Union Pacific near Dale Creek, Wyoming, in 1868 (page 53), is the earliest. These two photos bookend and represent the historical boundaries and technological evolution of the photographic work presented in *Railroad Vision*.

A little about our modus operandi. Due to time and financial constraints it wasn't possible to review all 120,000 images in the *Trains* files. Instead we opted for a "random-walk" approach—toggling between seeking out images of specific photographers, railroads, or regions while also electing to search the files with a spirit of adventure and no preconceptions, remaining open to whatever lay within them, awaiting dicovery.

And once we learned the language of the archive and began to inhabit the mind-set of George Drury—the man with the organizational brilliance to decide what went where and how—navigation became easier. But great, too, was our ability to stroll out of the archive and momentarily interrupt staffers Rob McGonigal, Kevin Keefe, or Jim Wrinn if we were stumped, searching for a particular image we'd previously seen but couldn't find. Their encyclopedic

knowledge of the files proved invaluable, especially when it came to locating the archive's more esoteric offerings.

Some of the research involved homework. We spent the better part of February and March 2014 chained to our Macs going through every issue of the magazine (as seen on Kalmbach's terrific DVD overview) looking for that obscure image to round out the selection. When we revisited the David P. Morgan Memorial Library in May 2014 we scoured the file folders once again to hunt down what we had discovered in the back issues of the magazine. Sometimes that proved successful, yet at other times the rare gem eluded us, a treasure left for a future researcher to unearth.

Some major revelations came our way. Most noteworthy perhaps were the photographs of Bruce Meyer: delicate exposures taken in soft eastern light, made into prints that were exemplars of darkroom craft (pages 21, 119, 138). Another extraordinary find was an album of photographs donated by the Illinois Central, created by a team of photographers who were commissioned to document the damage inflicted on the railroad by the 1912 and 1927 flooding of the Mississippi (pages 88, 89). Great pictures abounded from the "Kalmbach Crew" too: Wallace W. Abbey, Linn H. Westcott, W. A. Akin, and Al Kalmbach himself. One particular feature by Westcott, which was shot for an all-Monon issue of *Trains* in July 1947, was storyboarded with 2 x 2 prints glued down to scrapbook pages. Found neatly folded, theirs was a quiet residency in the file, pioneering examples of rail photojournalism long before anyone had uttered that phrase within the railfan world. One image from this series, modern and unconventional in relation to the accepted aesthetic of the times, shows its maker to be a visionary (page 16).

Lastly, we stumbled across a packet of 2¼ proof prints (pages 112–13) immaculately printed by Noel Hiram Deeks, the onetime assistant to the famed Photo-Secessionist photographer Edward Steichen. These diminutive prints from 1941–42 resonate with an aesthetic that not only echo the work done by Walker Evans a few years earlier but also anticipate the photographs emanating from

David Plowden's camera a decade and a half later. One wonders if Deeks was referencing Evans, or whether Plowden ever saw Deeks's previous work. Or was this all just coincidence?

It should be noted that we never intended this book, or this selection of photos, to represent "the best of" *Trains*. That would be hubristic at best. Who decides what's best? And based on what criteria? Instead we wanted to share with the viewer a survey of the archive's magisterial contents, to give you a sense of its diversity and totality. Within its resplendent confines there reside historical photos, examples of high art and bold aesthetics, moving journalistic imagery, human interest, and good straight-ahead railfan photography. The archive and this book provide an abundance of pictorial riches that we hope you'll find engaging, enlightening, and enjoyable.

WE'D LIKE TO EXTEND A HEARTFELT thanks to everyone at Kalmbach for their time, generosity, good cheer, and friendship. It was indeed our honor and great fortune to take this trip with Diane Bacha, Thomas Hoffman, Kevin P. Keefe, Diane Laska-Swanke, Rob McGonigal, and Jim Wrinn—a group of talented, no-nonsense professionals who aided and abetted us at every turn.

Lastly, we'd like to thank Jim Mairs, our esteemed and beloved editor at W. W. Norton and the Quantuck Lane Press, for his belief in this project as well as his lifelong passion for photography and the book arts. His dedication to publishing volumes celebrating the history of railroad photography has enlarged the breadth of our collective knowledge immeasurably. Jim, our admiration runs very deep.

A word from editor Jim Wrinn of *Trains* magazine

Railroad Vision is a compelling look back at steam locomotive photography in *Trains* magazine, founded in 1940. Today, seventy-five years and dozens of file cabinets later, *Trains* and our sister publication, *Classic Trains*, remain at the forefront of great railroad photography from across North America and around the world. Whether it's steam propulsion or any other type of locomotive or train, we cover them all, in print and on our website.

The tradition of great photography continues at *Trains*, as we mine a vast collection of carefully archived images—file folders stuffed with prints, binders brimming with slides, and digital collections committed to pixels. Railroad photography has never been more vibrant, thanks to digital cameras and inspired photographers who know the magic combination of railroads and light. On the page or on a computer screen, we're proud to offer images that evoke the grit, polish, and thrill of the railroading landscape as it continues to evolve.

Our promise to you is that the photographic legacy will continue, and we invite you to join us for the ride.

Jim Wrinn
Editor, *Trains* magazine

www.trainsmag.com
www.classictrainsmag.com

Trains

25¢
Canadian, 30¢

for NOVEMBER

Index